# The Great Adventure

## DEVOTIONAL

~

PATSY CLAIRMONT
BARBARA JOHNSON
MARILYN MEBERG
LUCI SWINDOLL
SHEILA WALSH
THELMA WELLS

TRACI MULLINS, *General Editor*

**W PUBLISHING GROUP™**

www.wpublishinggroup.com

*A Division of Thomas Nelson, Inc.*
*www.ThomasNelson.com*

Published by W Publishing Group, a division of Thomas Nelson, Inc., P.O. Box 141000, Nashville, Tennessee 37214.

Unless otherwise indicated, Scripture quotations used in this book are from the Holy Bible, New International Version (NIV). Copyright © 1973, 1978, 1984, International Bible Society. Used by permission of Zondervan Bible Publishers.

Scripture quotations noted NCV are from The Holy Bible, New Century Version, copyright © 1987, 1988, 1991 by Word Publishing, Dallas, Texas 75234. Used by permission; Scripture quotations noted KJV are from the King James Version of the Bible; Scripture quotations noted MSG are from The Message, copyright © 1993. Used by permission of NavPress Publishing Group; Scripture quotations noted NASB are from the New American Standard Bible, © 1960, 1962, 1963, 1968, 1971, 1972, 1973, 1975, 1977, 1995 by the Lockman Foundation; Scripture quotations noted NLT are from the Holy Bible, New Living Translation, copyright © 1996. Used by permission of Tyndale House Publishers, Inc., Wheaton, Illinois 60189.

**Library of Congress Cataloging-in-Publication Data**

The great adventure devotional / by Patsy Clairmont ... [et al.].
   p. cm.
  ISBN 0-8499-1775-1 (hardcover)
   1. Christian women--Prayer-books and devotions--English.
I. Clairmont, Patsy.
BV4844 .G75 2003
242'.643--dc21                                        2002015750

*Printed in the United States of America*

03 04 05 06 BVG 9 8 7 6 5

# Contents

PART 6

AIN'T NO MOUNTAIN HIGH
ENOUGH: DARE TO DREAM AND
DISCOVER

CONCLUSION

# OTHER BOOKS BY WOMEN OF FAITH

*Adventurous Prayer*
*Discovering God's Will for Your Life*
*Living Above Worry and Stress*
*Sensational Living in Jesus*
*Boundless Love Conference in a Box*
*Sensational Life Conference in a Box*

PATSY CLAIRMONT
*The Hat Box*
*The Shoe Box*
(both April 2003)

BARBARA JOHNSON
*Humor Me* (March 2003)
*Plant a Geranium in Your Cranium*

MARILYN MEBERG
*I'd Rather Be Laughing*
*The Zippered Heart*

LUCI SWINDOLL
*I Married Adventure*
*I Married Adventure Journal*

SHEILA WALSH
*Life Is Tough But God Is Faithful*
*Unexpected Grace*

THELMA WELLS
*Girl, Have I Got Good News*
*Bumblebees Fly Anyway*

# INTRODUCTION

## *Unchained*

### MARILYN MEBERG

~

THE GREATEST HAZARD IN LIFE IS TO RISK nothing," wrote an anonymous Chicago teacher. "The person who risks nothing, does nothing, has nothing, is nothing. They may avoid suffering and sorrow, but they cannot learn, feel, change, grow, love, live. Chained by their attitudes they are slaves; they have forfeited their freedom. Only a person who risks is free."

I wholeheartedly agree with those words. Some of us have the false notion that if we stay out of the thick of things we'll be safe. In doing so, however, we can become enslaved by that very source of so-called protection.

One of my favorite personalities has been the noted chef Julia Child. I remember as a little girl watching my father watch her on television. Her falsetto voice and peculiar intonations annoyed me; I didn't understand my father's enthusiasm. But Dad loved to cook, and gradually both my mother and I came to appreciate "the French Chef" as we sat down to Dad's various culinary experiments inspired by Julia's latest knife-wielding, small-pan-flipping recipes.

Julia Child's cooking suggestions provided great inspiration to me when I ultimately had my own kitchen. My efforts to impress Ken with my knife-wielding, small-pan-flipping recipes sprang from a sweet history. After my father died I was especially pleased to inherit his well-worn copy of *Mastering the Art of French Cooking* by Julia Child.

I was touched by an article I read about Julia as she spoke of her adventure of moving from her sprawling three-story house in Cambridge, Massachusetts, to a two-room apartment with a kitchen the size of a boat galley. The move felt like a huge risk to her. In spite of the risk, however, Julia's upbeat response to possible loneliness in her unfamiliar environment was: "I never feel lonely in the kitchen. Food is very friendly. Just looking at a potato, I like to pat it. There's something so pleasant about a big baking potato or a whole bunch of peas in their own shells. I'll be turning ninety soon and to me, the kitchen has never stopped being a place just full of possibilities and pleasures."

What an example of one who refuses to be "chained by her attitude." Many risks, like Julia Child's move, can be imposed upon us because of circumstances. Nevertheless, there is a choice to be made in whether we will risk being challenged—even invigorated—by the circumstances, or defeated by them.

My grandson Ian looked deeply into my eyes six months ago and told me he was about to have a new adventure, "but mostly he was scared" about it. With the divorce of his mommy and daddy, a move to Ohio made sense. Ian and Alec would have access to an enormous family of godly men, my daughter Beth could afford to buy a house for the three of them, and an excellent job waited for her that promised needed security.

Prior to their move last August, Ian and I had several chats about the risks he feared in a new school. What if the Ohio kids were mean? What if Ohio teachers were mean? What if his new neighbors were mean? (I thought the meanest thing he would encounter was Ohio weather, but I didn't bring that up.)

As I talk with Ian now, he never mentions mean kids, mean teachers, or mean neighbors, and apparently he hasn't found the weather mean either. He's mastering tae kwon do (yellow belt already), is excelling in school, and has settled into an interior place of new security and peace. In other words, "mostly I'm scared" about the Ohio adventure has proved worth the risk. He is "becoming, feeling, changing, and growing." I'm proud of him.

In this book my dear friends Barbara, Luci, Patsy, Thelma, Sheila, and I are going to be encouraging you to take a fresh look at your life, to ask some questions, take some risks, try out your wings in ways that perhaps you'd only dreamed of before. If such propositions trigger some "mostly I'm scared" responses, consider the words of the French novelist, Andre Gide, who said, "One doesn't discover new lands without consenting to lose sight of the shore for a period of time." And take comfort and joy in the words of the Jewish Savior, Jesus, who said, "I will never desert you." That divine promise enables each of us to lose sight of the shore and embrace the risks inherent in living free.

# Part 1

~c~

## YOU ARE HERE:

### WAKE UP TO
### YOUR SURROUNDINGS

# Just So Much Fluff

~

*This is what the LORD says:*
*". . . Ask where the good way is,*
*and walk in it." (Jeremiah 6:16)*

I AWOKE ON NEW YEAR'S DAY AND DIS-
covered I had been exceedingly generous to myself throughout the holidays. This was validated when I hefted my fluffy
body onto the scales and watched the numbers tally. I usually avoid instruments that measure my body parts, partly
because I don't want that much info and partly because I
have a strong aversion to numbers. I am a math misfit. I
much prefer words to numerical symbols—words are friend-
lier. And trust me, the sum total that glared up at me from
the scale window was not the least bit hospitable. Add to
that the problem with my jeans. Regardless of how I
stretched or pulled on them, they did not want to meet in
the middle and fasten.

"They must have shrunk," I told myself as I tugged on my
britches.

"Cheap fabric," I mumbled while I grappled with the snap.

"Faulty design," I gasped as I sucked in my breath.

Just the effort of snapping the denim shut caused a swell

of flesh to rise up and spill over the waistband. My midsection looked like a wave pool.

I could hardly continue to deny my dilemma with all that in-my-face information; I knew I needed a game plan. Unfortunately, my game plan didn't sound fun. Let me spell it for you: d-i-e-t. Been there? Done that? Me, too. Many times. So I should be an expert, but instead I tend to be a saboteur.

First I thought, *I shouldn't start my diet this week because I'm having a houseguest, and it wouldn't be friendly.* The following week I convinced myself I couldn't start then because I was going to fly west to our winter home in the desert, and travel is so disruptive to planned meals. Then I was busy settling into our condo, and I couldn't fit a food change into my busy days.

One morning I realized if I didn't just begin I would need to invest in an elastic company's stock. So I dragged my lagging attitude and my chubby carcass into my local diet center and started lifestyle changes. Besides consuming limited foods, I was encouraged to drink more water and to begin a walking program. Those two choices are not natural for me. But since I now had a financial investment in the program, as well as Cindy, a dear accountability person, to encourage me, I decided to give the changes an all-out effort. For ten days I obeyed the letter of the law. I ate only what was prescribed, I drank a lake, and I hoofed around my neighborhood.

Then came the weigh-in. I could hardly wait to be rewarded for my efforts. I slipped out of my shoes, hung my jacket over a nearby chair, and proudly stepped onto the scales.

Let me just say numbers are hostile and scales should be

limited to fish. I had lost three ounces. Yes, you heard me right, *ounces*.

"Ounces?" I wailed at the weigh-in lady. "Ounces? Why, I could shave my legs and lose three ounces!"

Cindy tried to encourage me. "Maybe you lost inches."

"A three-ounce inch?" I wasn't comforted.

When I arrived home still whining, a thought slowly dawned on me: I had felt much better those past ten days. And the walking had knocked some of my mental cobwebs loose. Not to mention the boost to my self-esteem that came as I made healthier choices.

I decided to risk the jeans test. I found them and wiggled my way into them. Guess what? They snapped! Of course I couldn't breathe or bend, but any progress was appreciated. I figure three ounces of my waist slipped down into my shoes, giving me just enough clearance to snap the jeans closed. But my loafers were tight.

The following week, even though I was traveling, I stayed on the program. It was an effort, inconvenient, and may I say, worthwhile. Because at the next weigh-in I had dropped three—no, not ounces—for-real pounds. Now I can even boogie in my jeans. Well, okay, maybe I don't boogie, but I can snap and breathe a little.

I figure at this rate that in another month or two, maybe three, I'll once again be able to wear the clothes in the recesses of my closet. But what feels even better is that I'm making good choices that are benefiting my overall well-being in the here and now. I'm so grateful I finally woke up and headed in a fresh direction.

Do you have anything in your life you need to face head-on? Relationship problems? Health issues? Disorders? Financial limitations? Take it from me: Dealing with reality can be a worthwhile adventure in itself—and today would be a grand time to begin anew.

~ *Dear Redeemer, gently awaken us that we might rise up and walk in the good way. Amen.*

# Pesto with Your Lemonade?

~

*We have different gifts, according to the grace given us.*
*If a man's gift is prophesying, let him use it in proportion to his faith.*
*If it is serving, let him serve;*
*if it is teaching, let him teach;*
*if it is encouraging, let him encourage;*
*if it is contributing to the needs of others, let him give generously;*
*if it is leadership, let him govern diligently;*
*if it is showing mercy, let him do it cheerfully. (Romans 12:6–8)*

CHRISTIAN AND I WERE SITTING OUTSIDE on a hot, muggy June day in Tennessee. The back of our house looks out on the sixteenth hole of a golf course, and we love watching the golfers make that tiny ball fly through the air like a nuclear snowball. It had taken Barry and me some time to persuade our enthusiastic son that his encouraging comments weren't always timely.

"This will be a good one!" he would cry out just as the golfer was about to strike.

"A bit higher!

"Use a bigger stick!

"You go, golfer!"

I'm sure that Christian is single-handedly responsible for

several hundred golf balls ending up in the lake. No wonder there are so many fish floating on top, concussed and confused.

This time he was being very quiet and respectful when the golfer broke the silence.

"Hey son, any lemonade up there?" the thirsty man called out.

"Sure thing," Christian replied, grabbing my glass and heading toward him with meaty resolve, the pale yellow liquid spilling all over the grass.

"Thanks, son, I was just kidding. It's kind of hot out here."

That evening while he was taking his bath I heard Christian relate the incident to his dad.

"When I was a little boy," Barry said, "I had a lemonade stand. One summer I made twenty-four dollars."

"Twenty-four dollars!" Christian cried out excitedly. "That's so cool. I'm going to have a lemonade stand, too."

The next morning he seemed to have forgotten about the idea, or so I thought.

"How many robots could you buy for twenty-four dollars, Mom?" he asked.

"A lot!" I said.

"How much would God get out of twenty-four dollars?"

"Well, at least two dollars and forty cents," I replied. "But we can give God more if we want to."

"So, God gets two dollars and forty cents and how much do I have left?" he said, ignoring my suggestion.

"Twenty-one dollars and sixty cents," I told him.

"Cool!"

The following week we were having dinner with Luci, Marilyn, Patsy, Thelma, and Women of Faith president Mary

Graham. It was a lovely restaurant with an extensive menu. At the end of the meal I saw Christian whisper something to our waitress. She smiled and nodded and disappeared into the kitchen. She came back a few minutes later and gave Christian a large sheet of paper folded in two.

"What do you have there?" I asked.

"I'll tell you later, Mom," he said.

That night as I was tucking him into bed he produced the sheet he had put under his pillow and gave it to me. I opened it up and saw that it was a copy of the menu from the restaurant.

"What's this for?" I asked.

"I'm serving food with my lemonade," he proudly announced. "Can you handle this, Mom?"

I looked down the list.

"Well, I'm not sure about the duck in a wild cherry sauce or the salmon with fennel or the sea bass with a crust of crushed almonds, but I could do the salad."

"All right, Mom. That's cool," he replied. "Can we do the pesto though?"

"Pesto! How do you know about pesto?" I asked.

"Luci told me it's good on penne pasta," he answered with all the confidence of a gourmet chef.

"It's green," I warned him.

"Gross! Forget the pesto. I'll stick with the lemonade."

One of the millions of things I love about my son is that he starts with what he has and does something with it. Sometimes the project is a success, sometimes a failure, but that never squelches his enthusiasm for the next endeavor. I often talk to women who want to do something adventurous for God but think that unless it's on a grand scale it doesn't count. I say, start where you are with what you have.

When people ask me how I got started as a singer I tell them that I began singing in hospitals and rest homes. With book projects, I began writing stories for my mom when I was a young girl in Scotland. I remember the first story I felt had achieved the status of a classic: "Joey the Budgie Was a Canary."

We place too much emphasis on ability when God looks for our availability to be used by him now, with whatever we have.

~ *Father, I offer myself to you today. Use me where you have placed me with what you have given me. Thank you. Amen.*

# Twenty-Year-Old Apple Pie

## LUCI SWINDOLL

~

*If you have faith as small as a mustard seed,*
*you can say to this mountain,*
*"Move from here to there" and it will move.*
*Nothing will be impossible for you. (Matthew 17:20)*

I ADMIT IT. I LOVE CELEBRATIONS . . . FOR any reason, anywhere. You name it, I'm at the dessert table, singing the loudest with my glass raised in salute. I like birthday parties, Christmas gatherings, anniversaries, and home-comings—anything that brings those I love into the same room together at the same time.

And for the record, I'd like to say I've received some marvelous gifts in my seventy-year span of celebrating. But one of my favorites came to me for Thanksgiving in 1999. My friend Kurt Ratican brought me eighteen apples—all individually and beautifully wrapped and carefully placed in a box. There was a note attached in his familiar scrawl:

*These are off the tree you planted in my backyard twenty years ago. Thought you might want to sample the fruit of your labor. Enjoy! With much love for the season, Kurt*

I could hardly believe my eyes. *Off the tree I planted?* I remembered that day in '79 so well. Kurt hadn't lived in his wonderful away-from-civilization house very long, but he owned enough property to have a garden and plant trees, flowers, and vegetables. He even had chickens, a duck, a dog, and two cats. Now that's all changed and he finds himself surrounded by numerous homes that dot the hillside and fill the landscape. There's little privacy left. But back then it was a quiet paradise, and I used to visit a lot.

I remember taking a shovel, digging just the right-size hole, and plopping that little apple tree in the ground. Kurt took a picture of me standing there, holding the shovel. My hair hadn't turned gray, no wrinkles were evident, and I was a shadow of my current self. More or less! Great big smile on my face because I had actually planted a tree, which I believed would one day grow into a giant. I looked smug and proud and happy—a farmer, wearing her overalls and a plaid shirt. It was a Kodak moment.

And now, here in front of me on my counter were apples from that baby tree of so many years ago. Nothing would do but to take a picture of *that*. I put all eighteen in a bowl, snapped the picture, then spent a couple of days communing with the apples, trying to think of a way to capture the memory for a lifetime. It suddenly hit me: *Make a pie, Lucille.* I had never made an apple pie in my life, but why not? My mother made pies, my brothers made pies, my friends made pies . . . why couldn't I? After all, I could farm; farmers made pies, didn't they?

I looked through a dozen books on pies, wanting this

thing to be the best ever. It was all so fun. Tunes from *Sweeney Todd* were bouncing in my head. I took pictures all along the way . . . before, during, after . . . and when the pie was baked and ready for consumption, I ate it all by myself over several days, enjoying every selfish bite. Each time I had a piece I celebrated again the day I planted that little tree and *this* day when I was enjoying its fruit. It was both Kurt's *and* God's gift to me. Thank you, Lord . . . for the tree, the apples, the idea, the pie, the photos, and the memories! The whole adventure is mine forever.

And there's a delightful irony as well: I got to know Kurt over a slice of apple pie. On the night we were introduced I liked him immediately. Knowing he lived just down the street from me, I asked if he'd like to come by my apartment for pie and coffee on his way home. He accepted and we visited for hours . . . laughing, swapping stories, getting to know each other. It was then I knew I had set in motion one of the sweetest friendships I would ever experience. In fact, a few years later I ran across an old ring that belonged to my great-grandfather and gave it to Kurt for his birthday. Inside I had these words engraved: *So glad you came up for pie.* We have come full circle, he and I, just like that ring . . . in a sweet, rich, forty-year relationship of love, tenderness, and adventure.

You may not know it, but right in front of you is an adventure waiting for you. It's in a tiny seed or thought, and it's yours for the taking. Some of the best gifts begin in the smallest, most inconsequential ways. Consider the size of a mustard seed. Or, in this case, an apple seed—very, very tiny, but in it there is enormous potential for growth. We might think that a particular idea or inspiration amounts to nothing, and let it lie dormant as a seed. But God encourages us to dig deeper, trusting that he will grow something wonderful. When we take the tiniest step toward welcoming growth, he brings the fruit. He produces an adventure worth savoring.

Go ahead—plant the seed. See what happens.

~ *Oh Lord, how wonderful to be alive in* this *moment. Thank you for the gift of this very second. Help me fill it with joy and gratitude and a creative idea. I believe you have something wonderful for me to discover whenever I'm willing to trust you for my next little step. I can't wait to see where you'll take me. Amen.*

# The Thrill of the Soup

## Barbara Johnson

~

*He took away your pride when he let you get hungry,*
*and then he fed you with manna, which neither*
*you nor your ancestors had ever seen.*
*This was to teach you that a person does not live*
*by eating only bread, but by everything the LORD says.*
*(Deuteronomy 8:3 NCV)*

ANYONE WHO'S ABLE CAN HAVE AN ADVENTURE if she's willing to set off toward the horizon, eager to explore new lands. But what about those of us who prefer to stay a little closer to home? What if we want to add a little excitement to our lives once in a while, too?

Over the years I've learned that adventure isn't just an odyssey. It's an attitude! For example, right after World War II, things were pretty tight financially for Bill and me. The nation had ended rationing for shoes, coffee, and sugar, but the prices still seemed sky-high. Many of us young couples who were beginning our families had to find ways to economize. We could have looked at the situation as a hardship, I guess, but instead we chose to consider it an adventure.

A big warehouse in our town sold excess or damaged containers of food for a fraction of the price we would pay in grocery stores. One of the best buys was the canned soup. You could buy a whole case of it for just pennies a can. For us, discovering that bargain was like finding the pot of gold at the end of the rainbow. We would buy a couple of cases and be thrilled to think we had gotten such a good deal.

There was just one catch: There were NO LABELS. Now, this could have been a big problem if the warehouse had distributed a variety of food items in these cans. But it was all soup—and it was *almost* all tomato soup! We could open up the can and trust that we would find tomato-soup concentrate that would provide us with a tasty lunch.

Occasionally, though, after twenty days or so of tomato soup for lunch, we would open a can and find split-pea soup instead. Now, split pea had not been a favorite flavor of mine when we began this soup regimen, but after days and days of nothing but tomato soup, it became a real thrill to have lunch that was green instead of red! I liked to think that whoever packed all those cans felt sorry for us thrifty soup shoppers and decided to toss in something different every once in a while as a little treat. If only he could have known how delighted we were to find that tasty surprise as the lid came off the can!

Remembering those days and recalling how tired we got of eating tomato soup every day (even with a few split-pea surprises thrown in), I can't help but think about the Israelites and how tired they must have grown of the manna God so graciously provided. Exodus 16:35 says they "ate manna forty years"! Can you imagine? But every morning, there it was again, waiting for them—waiting to provide nourishment and stamina to get through one more day in the wilderness.

God blesses us the same way. Sometimes he gives us just enough help to get through the next day—or the next moment. Sometimes his love seems like nothing fancy, just bare nourishment for our existence. Then something happens—something as simple as all the socks matching up when the laundry is folded, or something as wonderful as a comet streaking across a star-sprinkled sky—and if we're tuned in to God's love closely enough to perceive the wonder of it, our attitudes change. We might hear a child's laughter or feel a loved one's hand squeezing ours and suddenly feel overwhelmed with the abundant joy God provides us in our ordinary, humdrum lives.

These things have been there all along—the socks, the stars, the laughter, and the love—but maybe they seemed so plain and unremarkable, like a case of canned soup with no labels. What we have to remember is that in the plain everydayness of our lives, a million little blessings await us.

*⌒ Father, help me discover and appreciate the blessings that are waiting for me to find in each moment of every ordinary day. Amen.*

# Buried Bones

MARILYN MEBERG

~

*. . . Knowing that a man is not justified by the works of the Law but through faith in Christ Jesus. (Galatians 2:16 NASB)*

I CHUCKLED AS I READ A DESCRIPTION OF the ideal response to life. It is, the pithy prose claimed, the ability to start the day without caffeine; be cheerful regardless of aches and pains; gratefully eat the same food every day; take criticism and blame without resentment; relax without liquor and sleep without the aid of drugs. If you can do all this and more, the writer said, then you are probably the family dog.

Ah yes, the family dog. I well remember my sense of envy as our golden retriever, Chablis of Ambervale the Third, would amble through his days with not a hint of insecurity about anyone or anything. It never occurred to him it was beneath the dignity of his show-dog lineage to have fleas. Or that his ever-present offensive odor might frustrate the mother of the house who was known to run into the streets screaming, "How can you still smell when I just bathed you?!"

No, Chablis of Ambervale the Third never doubted his acceptability nor chafed under the nagging fear that his behavior was not good enough or his secret sins alienating to anyone, even the God of the universe. "Grace," he'd pant. "I'm one tail-wagging, food-scarfing, gas-expelling, bad-breathed, barking epitome of a grace recipient. So what's *your* problem, Mrs. Meberg?"

That lovable, furry package of maddening winsomeness had it right. He knew how to live without a sense of condemnation dogging his steps.

The good news is, I don't have to envy the family dog. I've got it made, too. I just can't seem to remember that. It's like I have a fantastic, too-good-to-believe bone, but I keep burying it, then digging it up, only to bury it again.

What is that fabulous truth I keep burying? *God loves me in spite of my offensive behavior.* He never runs into the streets screaming, "She still smells!"

So why am I forever digging a hole in which to bury such a simple and liberating truth? Here's my deal . . . maybe you can identify. I tend to reduce my relationship with God to bartering. I think, *I do for God; he does for me.* Bartered love means I assume God is pleased with me when I'm good, moral, and consistent. Based on his pleasure with my efforts, I'm rewarded. That faulty thinking leads me to try to live in such a way that he will love me rather than living in such a way because he already does.

The apostle Peter learned an agonizing lesson about bartered love. When he boasted to Jesus that nothing would ever wrench him from his Master's side, Peter was counting on his own determination at loyalty, his own gearing up of courage, and his inherent character not to crumble under personal threat. But not only did he crumble, he also, with repeated cursing, denied even knowing Jesus.

Peter was counting on his own efforts. He believed he could prove to Jesus that he was worthy of being a disciple. He believed that by behaving loyally and valiantly, his Lord would be proud of him . . . maybe love him even more. What Peter learned instead was that Jesus already loved him. Peter did not have to prove himself. In fact, he was not even capable of doing so. Peter, in his humanity, was weak, vacillating, frightened, and ultimately unsuccessful in living up to his ideals. He could not even barter; he was bankrupt.

Jesus knew all about Simon Peter. He knew that the same man who confidently declared, "You are the Christ, the Son of the living God" (Matthew 16:16), would deny him altogether when his fear got the best of him. Still, Jesus told his disciple, "Blessed are you, Simon son of Jonah, for this was not revealed to you by man, but by my Father in heaven. And I tell you that you are Peter, and on this rock I will build my church, and the gates of Hades will not overcome it" (Matthew 16:17–18). After the Resurrection, Jesus made sure Peter knew he was loved and forgiven in spite of his utter failure by appearing to Peter before any of his other disciples (see Luke 24:34). Peter learned that it was *only* the conquering love of God through Jesus on the cross and the ultimate infilling of the Holy Spirit that made Peter worthy of the name "rock." He had nothing to do with drumming up that image of strength. In his weakest moment he was anything but a rock. But God loved Peter even when he was reduced to crumbled fragments.

What was true for Peter is true for me. I'm not good at bartered love—all too often I'm also bankrupt. But God doesn't want to barter. In fact, ". . . God was reconciling the world to himself in Christ, not counting men's sins against them" (2 Corinthians 5:19).

So that, my friends, is my fantastic bone—my greatest treasure, right in the backyard of my own heart. In my quest for courageous, valiant, and adventurous living, I won't get far if I forget or bury that truth.

~ *Lord, thank you for your totally illogical but loving acceptance of me. Thank you that your love is too great to be wagered upon. Amen.*

# Fur-Felt Gratitude

## SHEILA WALSH

~

*Let the word of Christ dwell in you richly as you*
*teach and admonish one another with all wisdom,*
*and as you sing psalms, hymns and spiritual songs with*
*gratitude in your hearts to God. (Colossians 3:16)*

THOMAS O'MALLEY ADOPTED OUR FAMILY two years ago. I met him one night when I was taking out the trash. It was a cold January evening. As I turned to go back into the house I heard a faint meow coming from behind a bush. I peered inside the frost-encrusted bush and saw the head of a beautiful silver cat, his eyes riveted on me in obvious alarm. He darted out of the bush and disappeared into the night. The same thing happened a few nights later.

"I don't think that cat I told you about has a home," I said to Barry over supper. "Do you think we should leave some food out?"

"If you want another cat you should. Otherwise I wouldn't bother. If you feed a cat it tends to take it personally."

"But it's so cold," I continued. "I'll just leave a little food . . . and a box . . . and a blanket."

I put a bowl of tuna fish by the bush and sat and watched. The cat peered out, but when he saw me he disappeared again.

I went inside. The next morning the food was gone. I continued this for a couple of weeks. Eventually, he would come out and eat while I sat by the garage door.

Christian named him Thomas O'Malley, from the Disney movie *The Aristocats*. He was indeed an alley cat. Within a few months we were best of friends, and he had obviously adopted us as his family of choice. He would let me scratch him behind his ears, and he would rub up against my leg, purring like a little engine. When I sat out on the patio he would jump up and sit on my lap.

One morning I saw him sitting on the mat outside the back door. When I went out to feed him I saw that he had a huge cut all the way down his back exposing muscle and bone. I knew that he needed attention but wasn't sure how he would respond to being caught and put in a box to be taken to the vet. I was amazed, however, at how gentle and compliant he was as we picked him up and laid him on a towel in a box. The vet kept him for a week. He needed seventeen stitches and a course of antibiotics. He didn't seem to hold the ordeal against me. In fact, the morning after I brought him home and opened the back door to put food in his bowl, I saw he had left a thank-you present. There in all its glory was a dead mouse.

For the next week I dreaded opening the door. Some days it would be a mouse head or the back end of a mouse, an ear or two, whatever he could spare. Thomas was grateful and showed it. He has become the most delightful family pet. He is a huge cat, a regal animal, and gentle with all who show him kindness.

Adventure comes in many forms, but I've discovered that

what sweetens the whole journey is an adventure of the heart—one that can begin in each new moment. Expressing our gratitude to God is a rich adventure in itself. After all, think about what we've been delivered from. We've been rescued from the cold night of sin that alienates us from God. We were like strays struggling to keep warm, to find a place of shelter from the icy blast of life. We were hungry and naked, homeless and helpless, wounded and broken, marked by the scars of life. God in his overwhelming love sent Jesus to woo us back to God. He has paid for our healing; he fed us and loved us back to life. Now, a sweet part of our adventure here on earth is to live a life of gratitude.

I wonder if you are like me and forget sometimes what we have been saved from. Without this heavenly ransom we would still be lost and alone. We would have no future, no solid ground from which to launch into the many flavors of adventure life offers us. What better starting place in embracing adventure than in our own hearts. A dynamic internal miracle has already occurred because we have been rescued from the consequences of our propensity to go our own way and disappear into the night.

I am challenged by the gratitude of a stray cat that looks for ways to say "Thank you!" Let's enter into the love adventure of our lives and seek creative ways of telling our awesome God, "We love you! We thank you! We will live for you!"

~ *Father, there are no words to adequately express my gratitude for all you have done for me. You have saved me and given me a home forever. Thank you! Amen.*

# Recapture the Joy

## THELMA WELLS

~

*The joy of the LORD is your strength. (Nehemiah 8:10)*

THERE'S THIS GUY IN THE BIBLE THAT I visit fairly often. He's one of the coolest dudes I've ever gotten acquainted with. He's cool because he seems always to be focused and right on target regardless of what he's confronted with. Every time I visit him I see another intriguing quality that I missed the last time I went to his house. He lives in a chapter named for him found in the territory of the Old Testament, next door to his comrade Ezra and his boss's step-mother, Queen Esther.

"God is consolation." That's the meaning of his name. How cool is that? Nehemiah lived up to that name because whatever was going on around him, he'd turn to God and God would always give him consolation. Maybe that's why most of the time he had a great attitude, a smile on his face, and a passion for excellence. After all, he had a great job in the service of King Artaxerxes I Longimanus of Persia. The career was macho and dangerous, but Nehemiah was up for it. He was the cupbearer to the king, and his job was to sip the best wine from the vineyards and taste the most well-prepared and delicious food in the kingdom before the king drank or ate. The danger was, if the wine or food was poisoned, Nehemiah would get sick or die, thus preserving the health and life of the king. Not a problem for Nehemiah. His absolute confidence in his God made him all that and a bag of chips.

One day, however, Nehemiah got some disturbing news about his homeland and the conditions of the walls around Jerusalem. The walls of the holy city had been broken down, the gates were burned, and the people were in distress. This news troubled Nehemiah, and he wanted to fix everything for his countrymen. But as I said, he was cool. Instead of hurtling forward without being prepared, he mourned, fasted, prayed for direction from God, confessed and acknowledged the sins of his fellow Jews, reminded God of his promise to restore the Israelites, and asked God for success and favor with the king.

When he went into his boss's chambers one day, the king noticed that his cupbearer did not have the usual smile on his face and his attitude needed adjusting. This aroused the king's curiosity, and he asked Nehemiah what was wrong and what he wanted. Nehemiah was still cool. The brother did not answer the king until he whispered a prayer to God for wisdom. I'm sure Nehemiah's prayer was a fleeting thought or request. But when he did speak to the king, his words were from the heart of God.

The king responded with gracious favor and provided his cupbearer with rights of passage to go back to Judah, his motherland. Nehemiah's plan was to rebuild the walls and restore the city for the people. He had no architectural skills, no carpentry or masonry skills, but somehow he knew how to select the right team to work with him. At first he took three good men with him to check out the conditions of the walls and gates. But he didn't even let them in on what was really happening. He just told them, "The God of heaven will give us success" (Nehemiah 2:20). All during the rebuilding process, Nehemiah prayed to God and listened for his instructions. God protected the people as they worked like Trojans by day and guarded the city by night.

You can imagine that anywhere there is a group of people, somebody's going to get on edge and start expressing their opinions or needs. There were poor people in Jerusalem who had good reason to complain. When Nehemiah discovered their complaints were merited, he did something about it. He rebuked the countrymen who were taking advantage of the poor and asked them to make a vow that they would knock it off and make restitution. All the guilty got back on track, renewed their reverence for God, and became obedient to the God of their fathers. Throughout all this Nehemiah stayed focused on his primary task of rebuilding the walls and restoring the people.

His enemies plotted to kill him and sent him false truths via messengers of doom. They were trying to wear him down. But Nehemiah always remembered from where his strength came, and he prayed, "Now strengthen my hands, Lord." God did! Finally, the enemy lost confidence. Nehemiah finished the walls and gates in fifty-two days. But his work of restoration was not over.

In a census count of the inhabitants of Jerusalem there were more than forty-two thousand men, not counting the women and children. Their ancestors had been in Babylonian captivity for seventy years, and this was a new generation of citizens who knew little about their original homeland. In the town center a solemn assembly was called by Nehemiah, who was now the governor. Ezra, the priest and scribe, and the Levite preachers read the Law of God to the people and interpreted it so those who had long been in exile could understand. When the people heard what the Book of Moses had to say and realized what their relatives had done to get them sent away from their rightful land into bondage, the people were grieved and began to cry and squall with bitter tears. But Mr. Cool knew how to recapture their joy. I can just hear Nehemiah now—talking loud, but in a loving, tender, authoritative voice: "Don't cry on such a day as this! For today is a sacred day before the Lord your God—it is time to celebrate with a hearty meal, and to send presents to those in need, for the joy of the Lord is your strength. You must not be dejected and sad!" (see Nehemiah 8:9–10).

We can learn some valuable lessons from this brother about how to live effectively in our present circumstances, no matter what they are. Throughout his adventure with the king of Persia, the people of Judah, and his enemies, Nehemiah remained focused on the assignments God had given him. When things got rough or decisions had to be made, *he prayed.* He took his cues from the only Source that is all-wise and can never misguide or make a mistake. He remained in such close communication with God that he was given divine insight in the moment. He knew when trouble was around and the enemy was trying to trick him.

One of the things that inspires me most when I visit

Nehemiah is his joyful spirit. Throughout his adventure, he knew how to celebrate his accomplishments and see the good in what God was doing. The clincher was the big meeting in which folks tried to get all sensitive and emotional because of the past. They couldn't do nuttin' 'bout dat. They were home now. So Nehemiah put a stop to their whining before it got out of hand. He realized that if you feed folks and give them something to drink, add a little motivational speech, and get their minds on something larger than themselves, they can recapture their joy, even in the midst of sorrow.

Nehemiah kept his joy through all he experienced because he was constantly connected to the Joy Giver. Without God as your personal guide and consolation, there is no real joy in the adventure of life, only temporary happiness when things go your way. Your name may not mean "God of consolation", but you can enjoy the presence and direction of the One who is the Master Consoler, the One who can unleash wellsprings of joy in your heart and soul right where you are, right now.

*⌇ Joy Giver, just as you ministered to Nehemiah and your people throughout those weeks and years, you will do the same thing for us. Help us to rely on your promises, wisdom, comfort, and protection throughout each day we have on Earth. Show us how to recapture our joy. Amen.*

# Nab the Smack-Dab

## LUCI SWINDOLL

~

*In his heart a man plans his course,*
*but the LORD determines his steps. (Proverbs 16:9)*

I'M A PLANNER. ASK MY FRIENDS. WHEN I
get up in the morning, you can be sure my plan is in place. I
know what I'll do, when I'll do it, exactly how it'll be done, and
precisely how I'll celebrate when it's over. Interruptions, stay
out of my way. I have no interest in being bothered by *you*.

Typically, this works well for me. My friends envy my ability to plan and accomplish my goals. A plan and its successful
execution make me happy. I feel deeply satisfied in my soul.
Sometimes my plans are huge, like circumnavigating the
globe. More often, though, they're simple—like getting back
from the cleaners before *Law and Order* begins so I can enjoy
lunch and my favorite TV program at the same time.

There are occasions, however, when my perfectly laid plans
don't work for me. Why? Interruptions! Unexpected delays.
Circumstances out of my control. That's when I have to make
a choice—either lose my mind (and my decorum!), or look
beyond my puny plan and see if God has something different
or even better in store.

Flexibility doesn't come naturally to me. God has to bring

it about. And he keeps giving me opportunities to practice being flexible when things don't go my way. I continue to learn that some of the most memorable adventures are those smack-dab in the dailyness of life. Little surprise "detours" right in front of me, waiting for me to nab them for the delights that they are.

For example, recently I enjoyed an adventure that I had not planned or anticipated. After a Women of Faith conference, Marilyn and I were flying home to Palm Springs on a Sunday morning. It was the same weekend daylight-saving time went into effect, so all the clocks moved back an hour. We had taken a commuter flight from Indianapolis to Chicago, and as we disembarked we asked an attendant what time it was. She inadvertently gave us Indianapolis time instead of Chicago time, which was even later by an hour. We lolled around in the Chicago airport before going to the gate for our connecting flight. We made phone calls, had coffee, chatted . . . feeling glad about having such a long layover. It's wonderful not to rush—fits my style perfectly.

After a while, not wanting to hurry, I suggested to Marilyn, "Maybe we ought to mosey on down to the gate." Gathering up our things, we headed out. When we got there the information board read:

Flight #1136—BOSTON

Marilyn asked the attendant, "We're on the Palm Springs flight; was there a gate change?"

"No ma'am. That plane left thirty minutes ago. If you're going to Palm Springs, you missed your flight."

*We what?* Looking a bit confused, we asked the guy, "What

time *is* it, anyway?" When he told us and we finally came to our befuddled senses, we realized what happened and began to settle into reality. We were in Chicago—and who knew when we'd get out.

We talked with a ticket agent who began trying to reroute us. Embarrassed, we confessed our inability to tell time correctly, but her kindness and attentiveness saved the day. Even though almost every flight going anywhere was full, she found two seats to Dallas—leaving six hours later. From there we could get to Palm Springs. We'd be much older then, of course, but in unison we said, *Book it!* And she did.

I offered to buy Marilyn lunch. "Chicago pizza, anyone?" We both love Chicago pizza, and *in* Chicago? What could be better! We never have enough time to visit and never just "time on our hands." Who really cares if we get home in the middle of the day or the middle of the night? To linger over lunch for a change was wonderful, and we enjoyed a long, sweet visit. We caught up and laughed . . . continually asking each other, "What time is it? We have to catch a plane in six hours."

After lunch, we shopped, had our shoes shined, and wrote a postcard . . . chatting all the while.

Had everything gone according to our plan that day, Marilyn and I would have never had those delightful hours together. We would have missed the adventure. Had we gotten mad over what happened, we would have forfeited the most delightful part of the day.

God knows what we need better than we do. Sometimes he redirects our course, giving us a unique and unexpected treat—and meeting a need we didn't even know we had. Don't miss out on an unexpected treasure today by being too rigid. I've done that all too often—"gotta go, gotta do, gotta be"—when all the while God is saying to me, "Luci, I'm in charge. You've just gotta rest."

～ *Lord, you see the beginning, the end, and everything in between—and because you do I can trust you with my life. Guide me today where you want me to go, even if it means in a direction I never imagined. You are with me, offering me all sorts of unexpected treasures. Remind me to nab them along the way. Amen.*

# *Sprout!*

MARILYN MEBERG

~

*Delight yourself in abundance. (Isaiah 55:2 NASB)*

I GOT AN INSPIRATION THIS MORNING JUST as I was raising my sickle to slice a piece of Ezekiel bread for my morning toast. Though it drives me crazy, I tend to compulsively read whatever happens to be in my line of vision. Depending on my location, my reading can be as uninspiring as an ingredient label on a container of seasoning salt—or on my daily bread.

So what is Ezekiel bread anyway? Well, since you asked, it's 100 percent flourless bread purportedly inspired by the "recipe" in Ezekiel 4:9: "Take wheat, barley, beans, lentils, millet and spelt, put them in one vessel and make them into bread for yourself" (NASB).

Now before you dash out for a cup of spelt and a quarter-cup of millet, consider the secret to the recipe. We are advised (not from Scripture, but it still makes sense) that success lies in sprouting the grains before tossing them into the "vessel." Why? Because sprouting releases all the vital nutrients stored in each whole grain. (In case you wonder how I happen to be so well informed, it's because I read the side panel on the Ezekiel bread package while I wait for my toast. That's what they do with their grains. I've read that at least six times just this week.)

When the experts say that in order for us to experience optimum health benefits, the grains we consume must first "give off shoots and buds" (sounds slightly ominous), I'm inspired by the fact that each individual grain has sprout potential. All the grain needs is time and opportunity to do what it has the inherent capability to do.

*Surely, Marilyn, you're not going to compare us all to unsprouted grains that have yet to live up to their adventure potential.* Well, yes . . . that was indeed my breakfast inspiration. Bear with me. Isn't it just like God to place within all creation, grains or humans, the capability to sprout into life-enhancing richness?

A synonym for *sprout* that I particularly like is "burgeoning." It means to develop rapidly, to flourish. What energetic and compelling images! I wonder if God would not be pleased to see us literally burgeoning as we consider the subject of adventure. After all, he has created within each of us the capacity to thrive, as well as countless opportunities to do so right where we are. His desire is that we know burgeoning *abundance.* Jesus stated, "I came that they may have life, and have it abundantly" (John 10:10 NASB).

Perhaps not knowing that God indeed wishes abundance for us may be one reason we don't sprout. Instead, we slog through our days, doing our duty for God and country, asking the age-old question, "Is this all there is?" The answer? There's *more.* That more includes the freedom to enter into a lifestyle of God-inspired adventure because there is abundance there.

Now here's an example of what I'd call God-inspired adventure. A headline in my *Jesus Film Project Update* magazine proclaimed, "Run for the Son Funds Evangelism." What . . . ? In the article I learned that for fourteen years the Christian Motorcyclists Association has sponsored an annual 100-mile ride that helps raise funds for Bibles as well as for promotion of the *Jesus* film, a widely influential evangelism tool. Talk about burgeoning! If you don't want to *vroom-vroom* on your own motorcycle, you can pledge money on someone else's and help to raise a fortune. As a result of Run for the Son, the Jesus Film Project has financed film teams in Kenya and Uganda and purchased four-wheel-drive vehicles and equipment sets for both countries. Wow!

A lifestyle of God-inspired adventure may be as quiet as writing a check for a worthy cause or hopping on a motorcycle and taking off on a Run for the Son fund-raiser yourself. Whatever the chosen activity, it need not be dull, boring, tedious, or routine. As long as we know that we have sprout potential, there's no stopping us!

Maybe all we have to do is wake up to our surroundings, listen to the interior prompt that assures us we can sprout, and we're off and *vroom*ing. C. S. Lewis said, "The future is something which everyone reaches at the rate of sixty minutes an hour, whatever he does, whoever he is." So let's not just sit in our vessels; instead, let's grab a slice of fully sprouted Ezekiel bread and join the action. The clock is ticking.

∼ *Lord, help me to have a spirit of courage and not timidity. You have provided abundance. Remind me to live in that. Amen.*

# Color Me Amazed

PATSY CLAIRMONT

~

*No eye has seen, no ear has heard,*
*no mind has conceived what God has prepared*
*for those who love him—but God has revealed*
*it to us by his Spirit. The Spirit searches all things,*
*even the deep things of God.*
*(1 Corinthians 2:9–10)*

MY HUSBAND, LES, IS THREE PAINT SPLOTCHES short of a full palette. No, not mentally. Mentally his box of crayons is complete, but colorwise he's missing . . . well, for one, *red.* The man can't see red. Oh, trust me—he can heat up under the collar. But he can't distinguish the color red from, say, green.

In fact, most of life is green to Les. In the splendor of a Michigan autumn, when I point out a flaming-red maple tree, he can't tell the difference between it and the evergreen next to it. That makes me sad because red comes in such dramatic hues, and I want him to experience the full impact of autumn or anything else dressed up in crimson (like me).

Les also can't distinguish grays and browns from each other, and pinks appear green. So he needs help to select his daily attire, lest he appear in public looking overly festive. I've tried to simplify his wardrobe so everything is mix and match, resolving most potential dressing fiascos.

In contrast to Les's missing Crayola, my friend Jackie Edmons told me an unforgettable color story about her dad, John S. Thoman. John worked in the field of paint and wallpaper and had a gifted eye for color. He quickly learned to identify hundreds of colors. John also could tell you, by eying a swatch, which paints were needed to create a particular shade. Now, that's impressive. Today we have color machines to decipher measurements of each color necessary to achieve a match, but John was a human color machine.

At the age of sixty-five, John became seriously ill and slipped into a coma. His family was called in because he wasn't expected to live; they were instructed to bring their funeral clothes. After they gathered, to the amazement of family and doctors, John suddenly woke up. And equally stunning was the Technicolor adventure he recounted.

John had found himself, while in the coma, chest-deep in a manicured garden of flowers. The blooms were colors he had never seen before. As he studied their beauty and vibrancy, he realized he had no idea what one would mix to make any of the colors. After awakening he shared that the colors defied description because nothing on Earth could compare to them.

John said he would be standing in the garden, and then everything would turn black. Then he would find himself back in the garden again, only he would be closer to a city. This happened repeatedly until, almost to the city gates, he suddenly woke up in his hospital bed.

That same day, as John's pastor was preaching his Sunday

evening sermon, he stopped and told the congregation they needed to pray for John. This was not the norm for the minister, especially midway through a message. The pastor told his people, "We need to turn our pews into altars and lift our friend to the Lord." And so they did.

Early the following morning the family filed in to say their good-byes. Instead of finding a comatose patient hooked up to multiple machines, much to their profound surprise they found John sitting up in bed, machine-free, eating breakfast.

John's story takes my breath away. I have thought of it again and again through the years. Years that have, at times, been gray with grief. When I would remember John's garden of colors beyond human comprehension, shades of hope would trickle into my soul. I've also had a lot of indigo days in which an inexpressible sadness would color my outlook. Indigo, while lovely in a stained-glass window with the light filtering its hues, is hard to see through when it is one's only perspective. And I've experienced fleeting, rose-colored moments when all seemed well with the world.

Sometimes I forget Earth is not the last statement. In fact, it's really the parentheses. But that's hard to hang on to when one is sloshing around chest-deep in the here and now. Then I lift my eyes to the ebony skies lit with sterling stars and an ocher moon pillowed in velvet, and I'm reminded of the Creator and his unimaginable palette. Or times when the sunrise scatters amber shafts across my pillow, which warm my heart with thoughts of the morning when we shall awake at the gates of the city—and the Great Adventure will actually just be beginning.

*~ Lord God, we are in awe of the way you have colored creation. We can't imagine your future palette. When the veil is finally drawn back and we view what you have prepared for those who love you, I can only believe that we will fall on our faces in worship and fullness of joy. Amen.*

# Part 2

~c

## A Fork in the Road:

### Take it

# Pink Pigs

## MARILYN MEBERG

~

*See, I am doing a new thing!*
*Now it springs up; do you not perceive it?*
*I am making a way in the desert*
*and streams in the wasteland. (Isaiah 43:19)*

MY FAVORITE DEFINITION OF *ADVENTURE* IS "AN undertaking of uncertain outcome." I had one of those when my dear friends Luci Swindoll, Mary Graham, Ney Bailey, and I went on a cruise through New Zealand and Australia.

Incidentally, there is a disadvantage to traveling with me. I hate to shop! I try not to whine or fuss, but one day I was overcome. I'll tell you about it because it led to one of the greatest adventures of my life.

In every port we hired a driver to take us to local points of interest. Invariably, those points included gift shops. Within a short time I'd fingered and evaluated the lanolin content of every wool product in New Zealand.

On the fifth day of our trip we were on a huge kiwi farm, which included cows, chickens, and sheep. Seeing how kiwis grow takes little time or study. So what else do we do? You got it: The gift shop was located at the edge of the farm next to a pen of very cranky goats.

I sidled over to Vicki, our driver. "I may lose my mind . . . break out in huge hives or take off my clothes and run shrieking about the cow pasture." (Imagine how that could throttle the milk supply.) Surprisingly, she not only understood the cause of my breakdown, but she had a solution. With a mischievous glint in her eye she said, "Come on—you need a dose of Hill Hoppers." Instantly I calmed down and agreed, not having a clue what a dose of Hill Hoppers entailed.

Not far from the gift shop was the "House" where little four-wheel-drive open-topped Suzuki trucks complete with roll bars were for rent. One could drive them through the "bush-clad" hilly terrain of the kiwi farm. The little trucks were called Hill Hoppers Fantastic.

I was soon sitting in one of those wet, muddy vehicles being outfitted with an enormous crash helmet and strapped into an unnecessarily ambitious harness with double straps over both shoulders as well as a huge strap across my middle. Mercy!

Luci leaped into the seat beside me with a hurried "I'm not letting you do this alone, babe—it looks rough!" Rough? After she'd harnessed and helmeted, we were introduced to Cindy, who would be in the lead vehicle shouting instructions from her CB radio to ours. Instructions?

Cindy got into her truck and took off. The words "Gun it" came crackling through our CB. Saying "Gun it" to Marilyn is like saying "Sic 'em" to a dog. We peeled out, lurching wildly from left to right as I tried desperately to maneuver the deeply and unevenly rutted tracks in the dirt (mostly mud) road. Never once did it occur to me to take my foot off the accelerator until Cindy instructed me to halt.

Luci and I were still shrieking with laughter over our out-of-control gyrations when Cindy put a blindfold on me. She told me to drive until she instructed me to stop.

"What?" I protested. "I can't see a thing!"

"That's the point. Luci will voice-guide you."

More wild driving, more hysterical laughter, until my passenger's "Go right—no, more right" ran us into a tree. Luci then took the blindfold as well as the wheel. More wild driving and hysterical laughing. I guided her into several bushes, but we avoided the trees.

After I resumed my rightful place behind the wheel, Cindy said, "Okay—are you ready for the big one?"

"The big one???"

"Yes, we're doing twelve adrenaline-pumping challenges on this course. This is the big one."

*Wait a minute,* I thought. *I was just going to toodle around the hills in a muddy truck. I didn't realize I was doing an obstacle course.* I asked Luci if she was game for whatever. Still giggling from the blind ride, she encouraged me: "Let her rip, Marilyn."

"All right," Cindy said, "you see the pink pigs on either side of the road just ahead?"

"Pigs . . . I don't see any pigs . . . I see cows . . . no pigs!"

"Pegs, Marilyn, pegs!" Luci hissed. "There are no pigs!"

"Why can't she speak clearly?" I hissed back.

"It's her accent, Marilyn. She *lives* here, in New Zealand. Remember?"

Cindy told us that as soon as she passed the marker pegs her vehicle would immediately disappear from view. Jumping into her truck, she sped past the "pink pigs" and literally disappeared. Almost immediately we heard "Gun it" on our CB. Not having a clue what was beyond the pegs, I gunned it. Within seconds we were catapulted into space . . . it must have looked like the final scene in *Thelma and Louise*. Screaming at the top of our lungs, we plunged back to Earth with bone-jarring abruptness. We were so exhilarated we couldn't stop high-fiving each other as we "gunned it" through the rushing, muddy water of a river called "Te Puke."

After brilliantly completing our "challenges" and hurtling back to Hill Hopper House, Luci said, "You know, Marilyn, we could have been killed! What if we'd hit those road ruts wrong when we crash-landed. We could have rolled—been crushed."

"Not a chance," I said humbly. "I was driving."

This wild down-under adventure was a "sweet Jesus" touch for me. Whenever I recall it, I'm encouraged never to think my life is over until it's over. I never know what's just around the bend.

You may be weak, sick, discouraged, or depressed. God may not be done with you. You just might see a crash helmet waiting for you down by a fork in the road.

~ *Lord, your road is paved with love and grace as well as adventure. Help me to never miss the markers. Amen.*

# Loosening My Grip

PATSY CLAIRMONT

~

*I will fear no evil, for you are with me. (Psalm 23:4)*

MY PLAYFUL HUSBAND HAS A TELESCOPIC TABLE fork that he loves to operate during company whenever we have dinner guests. A real conversation piece, you say? Oh, please. It looks normal enough until he spots food across the table that he would like, usually on someone else's plate. That's when the fork is extended out, out, out, until Les nabs a biscuit or a potato, and then he retracts the handle, bringing the tasty tidbit safely to his plate.

I, too, have forks—a whole collection. Not retractable ones, not even sterling ones, but the fork-in-the-road kind. Besides being an agoraphobic, I had multiple fears. Eventually, with each fear, I would come to a fork in the road, and I would have to choose which way to go—deeper into my fear or toward healing.

During my twenties, I stopped riding in cars unless I absolutely had to. I found it difficult to trust someone else's driving, which left me tense and on the verge of panic while in transit. And I sure didn't want to be the driver—I was too nervous, and I had lost all confidence in myself.

My belief that I should feel confident before I chose to trust the Lord or anyone else slowed my return to a functioning lifestyle. Gradually, I realized that my feelings couldn't be relied on to be rational. After all, my emotions weren't designed to reason but to feel. If I were to become mobile again, I would need to take a step of faith and face my fear, taking the fork in the road toward a healthier mentality.

The day I became a willing passenger was a major step in the right direction. For a while, even after I began to ride regularly in cars, when I'd step out of the vehicles, deep grooves were visible in my palms from my fingernails as my fists had tightened with tension. I would literally have to pry my fingers from their curled positions. I then began to practice relaxing exercises as I rode by willing my hands to loosen up, and after a time of learning how to monitor my body's stress, I became more comfortable.

But just when I finally could breathe easy on the highway of life I spotted—yikes—another fork in the road. This time I had to decide whether I would slip behind the wheel and drive myself to town (three miles away). It sounds so simple, yet I was terrified.

Some days I did better than others. I was no overnight success, but I kept at it until I was darting around town in my little jalopy. Go, girl! A megavictory for me came when I drove my aging mom and aunt from Michigan to Kentucky.

Taking a fork in the road spells "adventure" to some and "danger" to others of us who appreciate predictability, even if it is a measurable rut. Learning to be adventuresome again (I had been as a youngster) included lessons for me on taking the risk of trusting others, the Lord, and myself.

I gained strength for the challenge as I studied the lives of God's people, people who shook in their sandals and yet still obeyed God's direction. When they came to a fork in the road, they depended on him to direct their steps, whether they found themselves in a desert, a furnace, a prison, or a shipwreck. And there were those who were too afraid initially to take God at his word: the Gideons and the Peters. Yet God gathered their weakness into his strength and sent them forth with courage. That gives me hope that even in my most inadequate moments, when I'm tight-fisted with fear, the Lord still reigns over my life.

Recently, Sheila selected magnets as gifts for Luci, Marilyn, Thelma, Barbara, and me. She spent time searching for just the right ones, ones that would suit each of us. We oohed and ahhed over her choices. Mine was a quote by Eleanor Roosevelt: "Do one thing every day that scares you." And that quote, folks, sums up how I finally escaped the prison of my mind and my home. I chose the right, scary fork.

> The LORD is my light and my salvation—
> whom shall I fear?
> The LORD is the stronghold of my life—
> of whom shall I be afraid? . . .
> For in the day of trouble
> he will keep me safe in his dwelling;
> he will hide me in the shelter of his tabernacle
> and set me high upon a rock. (Psalm 27:1, 5)

*~ Our heavenly Father, you knew life could be scary. I read repeatedly in your Word the phrases "be not afraid" and "fear not." Thank you for understanding that we constantly need reassurance. Thank you especially for your unretractable love. Amen.*

# Chasing Pots

## THELMA WELLS

~

*Taste and see that the LORD is good;*
*blessed is the man who takes refuge in him. (Psalm 34:8)*

WHEN I THINK ABOUT A FORK I SELDOM
think about a fork in the road. I think about a fork in my
mouth. I know what "fork in the road" means: it's an opportunity to change. So, let me tell you about an opportunity to
change that came my way very early in life.

You've heard about the proverbial pot of gold at the end of the
rainbow. When I was a young girl, that was a common expression. It was meant to encourage us to work hard, doing all we
could to get rich, successful, happy, or whatever we thought were
the goodies in the pot waiting for us at the end of our efforts.

Now, looking for the "pot of gold" can sometimes be a
noble enterprise. But from my earliest memory, I found myself
chasing quite different pots: pans, skillets, cookie sheets, and
grills, to be exact. I would place the goodies from those pots on
plates, saucers, cups, and bowls, and my best friends were the
forks or spoons that were jet-propelled from those goody hold-
ers to my mouth. Chasing food became a great adventure.

My pot-chasing days started when I was a little girl at my
great-grandmother's table where breakfast was a must. Bacon,

eggs, grits, toast, pancakes, waffles, homemade jelly, butter, juice, and milk were an everyday beginning. Lunch was a meat sandwich with everything but the kitchen sink or some kind of homemade soup or stew. And dinner was always three courses, often with several dishes like chicken-fried steak, ham, roast, lamb chops, turkey, oxtails, neck bones, fried chicken, mashed potatoes, corn, collard greens, turnip greens, mustard greens, string beans, new potatoes, sweet potatoes, squash, macaroni and cheese, black-eyed peas, homemade rolls, corn bread, butter, jelly, and a scrumptious dessert.

No wonder I chased the contents of the containers on the stove. The stuff that was served up from them was too good to let spoil. I took my eating instructions seriously. "Eat all your food. I ain't got food to throw away!" So rather than be scolded for not eating with gusto, I gladly obliged.

Chasing pots and pans brought predictable results. Pouring in all those goodies made me a statistic of obesity at the age of nine. I was so fat that the doctors at Freeman's Clinic in Dallas had to put me in the hospital and reduce me to my normal weight. A layer of fat had covered my heart, and I had become a candidate for living above the rainbow in the Third Heaven, never to chase another pot again.

Within ten days, under medical supervision, I started to feel like a little girl who could more easily run, jump, and enjoy breathing when I played. After that fork in the road, my great-grandmother altered her feeding style dramatically. I kept my weight normal until I had my first child.

When people told me I needed to eat for two, I took them literally. After my baby was born, I had all but doubled my weight. I hated the way I looked. During my pregnancy, the pleasant adventure of eating properly was sidetracked by erroneous urgings and emotional yearnings, and I ended up taking the road that led to depression, shame, guilt, and severe obesity. Through tears, anger, frustration, and intimidation I tried every suggestion given to me to lose weight. Consequently, I went to fat doctors and took shots and pills. You name a diet I haven't been on and I'll give you a nice gift. Every day in every way I struggled with my weight. I lost count of how many times my feelings were hurt by people who would say things like, "What happened to you?" "I didn't recognize you." "You don't look like yourself." "What are *you* doing to lose weight?"

I did lose weight with the shots, pills, and diets. But the disastrous result was depression one minute and mania the next. I was agitated most of the time. And every time I'd get off the pills or diet, I would gain back even more weight than I'd lost. I was headed straight to the end of the road of health, and I didn't know how to take the better fork.

Today, at over sixty years of age, I've finally found a recipe in the weight-loss/get-healthy pot that's made a difference in my life. The fork is now pointed in the right direction for me. I received great advice from my daughter Vikki after she and others had tried Dr. Peter J. D'Adamo's "eating right for your blood type" approach with stunning success. Actually, it's the most sensible and easiest eating arrangement I have ever tried. I'm eating almost all the fruits, veggies, fish, whole-grain breads, and other delicious foods I want. Eating has become an adventure again, but this time the results are positive: I'm more mentally alert, have more energy, and experience less stress. I've reduced my cooking time, my skin is clearing, my eyesight has improved, my hypertension is stabilized, and I've lost weight without really thinking about it.

Take it from me: Chasing the fat found in the pots on the stove will leave you feeling frumpy, fit to be tied, and fighting back tears. But there is another pot that contains all the fixings of the true fulfillment we seek. Although the contents of this pot can cause growth and increase, these goodies never make us obese. Quite the contrary: The more we eat, the more we need to eat. The ingredients feed our spirit, mind, and soul. When consumed correctly, the goodies in this pot never cause depression, stress, anxiety, agitation, aggravation, anger, or anything distasteful or destructive. We can eat this food any time of day or night without regretful results. We never have to put a lid on this pot or place where it won't spoil. It remains fresh day after day, year after year. Everybody's blood type is completely compatible with the contents of this pot. No more dieting. No more deprivation. No more disillusionment. All we have to do is dip into the pot, ladle out what we want to chew on, swallow it, let it grow on us, then share it with someone else. The brand name of this pot is the Holy Bible. I call it the Pot of Testaments.

When you come to a fork in the road, take it, taste it, try it. You'll like it!

~ *Lord, no matter where we are on our journey, help us to realize that you have the recipe for cooking up everything we need to eat along the way. Amen.*

# Forkfuls of Delight

## MARILYN MEBERG

~

*Your words were found and I ate them, and your words became for me
a joy and the delight of my heart. (Jeremiah 15:16 NASB)*

SOME OF MY GREATEST ADVENTURES HAVE BEEN
taking the fork that leads me to food. Many of these fork trails
have led to foods of unknown origin. For example: the Waldo
Burger. Not many miles from where my daughter Beth lives in
Marion, Ohio, is the little town of Waldo where the Waldo
Burger originated. On my first visit to Ohio I was told I must
have a Waldo Burger. I agreed, though I had no idea what it was.

At my insistent urging, Beth's biological parents (Steve and
Sherry Boothe) took Beth and me to Waldo. There on the street
corner was a dilapidated tavernlike building with a badly painted sign boasting "Home of the World-Famous Waldo Burger."
As we walked into the "Tavern," I noted scruffy-looking people
sitting on tall stools slugging down some beverage from a long-
necked bottle. Tremulously, I asked Steve, pastor of a Baptist
church in Marion, if he should be in a tavern. He laughed and
assured me we were not in a tavern even though it looked like
one. Because of the scruffy-looking children sitting at red-
oilcloth-covered tables I assumed we truly were not in a place
that would interfere with our sterling Christian witness.

Our burgers accompanied by batter-fried cauliflower hearts were served by a waitress with dirty fingernails who appeared old enough to have just completed the fifth grade. The burger was served on a round paper plate only slightly larger than the sandwich itself. In order to secure each burger to the plate the baby waitress pressed the middle of each bun with her thumb. (She could only serve two at a time with that strategy but nothing slipped from position, including the two sweet pickles held by her little finger.)

I found the ludicrousness of this whole experience beyond my self-control and began giggling. Beth was embarrassed by my behavior, the waitress was puzzled, and Steve and Sherry smiled indulgently. I guess the bun-thumb indention was funny only to me.

By the way . . . let me tell you what a Waldo Burger is. It's a round slab of bologna about a quarter-inch thick. I think the culinary trick is to fry the bologna and place it immediately into a cold bun, which has just been pulled from its cellophane package. Whatever the secret, I loved it and would go back to Waldo in a heartbeat.

At the opposite end of the culinary spectrum was the meal some of us Women of Faith persons had at a very upscale French restaurant called Le Bec-Fin in Philadelphia. For an hors d'oeuvre I ordered *Cou d' oie farci,* which I later learned is stuffed gooseneck. That, of course, brought up troubling images. There's something about a goose that's always appealed to me. Nibbling on its neck seemed disrespectful to the poetry of the esteemed Mother.

For an entrée I ordered adventurously, but unwisely:

*Pigeons aux petits pois* (pigeon in peas). Whatever was I thinking? I've never seen a bird that looks more mentally vacant or aimless in its wanderings than a pigeon. It does not trouble me when they congregate mindlessly on my roof, but how could I possibly order one for my plate? (I ate the peas.)

For dessert my spirit soared as I dived into *Profiteroles au chocolat.* These are little pastry puffs filled with confectioners' custard and then smothered in hot chocolate sauce. I also ate Sheila's dessert, since she was full and I had hardly eaten anything. Her dessert order was *Gâteau basque:* custard flavored with vanilla and spread over a flaky crust. I loved the desserts at Le Bec-Fin as much as I loved the Waldo Burger.

Probably my very favorite fork trail was the one that led me to the home of Thelma Wells. She had been telling us for months that she was going to have a soul-food dinner at her house just for us speakers and our helpers. We fussed until she finally came up with a workable date. Well now, let me tell you—I thought the Lord had come and taken a minute to eat before we were all raptured off the earth. I can go a lifetime without ever establishing a relationship with collard greens and okra, but Thelma's macaroni and cheese . . . now, that's heaven! Because I kept replenishing my plate (the fried chicken was also to die for), Patsy and I nearly locked forks in a fight for the finish of the macaroni. She loved it as much as I.

Though fried bologna, French desserts, and Thelma's macaroni and cheese inspire great joy in the heart of anyone who appreciates "the fork," God maintains that his words are even more delectable. He not only told Jeremiah about the joy of eating the divine words, but he also instructed Ezekiel on the same subject. God said, "Son of man, feed your stomach and fill your body with this scroll which I am giving you" (Ezekiel 3:3 NASB). Ezekiel's response? "Then I ate it, and it was sweet as honey in my mouth."

Ah yes . . . the sweet words of the Father . . . the ultimate menu from which I want always to have my soul's palate delighted, my appetite satisfied, and my fork poised in a position of readiness.

~ *Father, feed me till I want no more. Amen.*

# The Grace of a Near Miss

BARBARA JOHNSON

~

*A father to the fatherless, a defender of widows,*
*is God in his holy dwelling. (Psalm 68:5)*

MY MOTHER HAD COME FROM MICHIGAN to visit us in our southern California home, and I wanted to show her a good time. So, on a hot summer day, we set out on an adventure: a visit to the *Queen Mary,* the luxurious cruise ship that was temporarily docked at Long Beach, about twenty miles away. Bill and the oldest boys stayed home, but our youngest son, Barney, came along with Mother and me.

Lots of people had the same idea we did that day, all drawn by their curiosity to see the famous ship. We had to park quite a distance away, so by the time we got to the ticket booth, we were already tired. Standing on the dock alongside the huge vessel, we craned our necks back and stood in awe of how high its upper decks soared above us, how numerous were its portholes and lifeboats. Then we began our exploration.

We decided to start at the top deck and work our way downward. So we crossed the boarding ramp and headed up the first of several flights of stairs. It seemed as though we climbed forever, and I was worn out from trying to help Mother navigate the steep stairways while also keeping Barney from scampering up the steps and disappearing from sight. Finally, we climbed the last set of stairs, waited forever for an elevator, and then emerged into the glorious sunlight of the top deck. We settled into the sun-drenched deck chairs and enjoyed the pleasant breeze that tickled the flags framing our spectacular view of the Long Beach harbor.

Suddenly I heard my name booming from the loud-speaker: "Barbara Johnson! Barbara Johnson! Please come to the *Queen Mary* ticket booth immediately for an emergency message." The announcement was repeated several times, nearly paralyzing me with shock and fear. Remembering how long it had taken me to get up all those stairways with Mother and Barney, I couldn't bear the thought of shepherding them both back down as I tried to rush to the ticket booth. So I left Mother in charge of Barney and hurried back down, alone, to the ship's exit and then back out on the dock to the ticket booth.

As I ran, I prayed, "Lord, please don't let it be Bill and the boys. Please, Lord, don't let it be my family. Please let them be safe. I can handle anything else, just not my family. Please, Lord, I beg you. But if it's bad news, Lord, I know you'll see me through it."

Finally, nearly out of my mind with anxiety, I rushed up to the ticket booth and gave my name.

"Mrs. Johnson, I'm so sorry. There's been a call for you. Your father has had a stroke and has been taken to a hospital in Long Beach," the attendant told me sympathetically.

"My father? Oh, thank goodness," I breathed out a great sigh of relief.

"Excuse me?" the woman said, obviously shocked at my response.

"I'm the wrong Barbara Johnson. My father died thirty years ago," I panted, still winded from having run down all the staircases.

I allowed myself just a few moments to collapse onto a nearby bench before heading back up to where Mother and Barney waited, full of worry, on the top deck. "Thank you, Lord," I prayed.

And then I thought of the other Barbara Johnson, whoever she was, still somewhere on the ship, hurriedly making her way to the ticket booth with the same fearful trepidation I had felt just a few moments earlier.

"Give her your strength, dear Jesus," I whispered. "Hold her up as she hears this news, and keep her in your loving embrace as she faces whatever lies ahead."

I raised my head and peered up at the huge ship again. "And Lord, if you could help me climb all those stairs again, I'd be forever grateful."

To be honest, I don't remember much about the *Queen Mary*. After I made my way back up the long staircases again, I shared the good news with Barney and Mother, and we sank back down onto the deck chairs to enjoy a moment of thankful relief. Then we ambled around the ship for a while, admiring the well-appointed staterooms and the opulent dining rooms. I know we saw those things, but I don't remember them. The only thing on my mind at that point was getting back home to Bill and our three older sons, throwing my arms around them, and reminding them all how much I loved them.

Sometimes it takes a crisis to help us remember what's truly important in our lives. Sometimes we look back and see a hard turn when our journey took on a new direction or a new emphasis. That fork in the road might come as a result of something wonderful, like getting married, or something tragic, like the loss of a loved one. Or we might see that our lives were enriched by a near miss with tragedy, as mine was that day.

There would be times in the years ahead when the bad-news message *was* for me: when two marines in dress uniforms came solemnly to my door; when a phone call from the Canadian police interrupted our family's dinner with devastating news; when a doctor stood at my hospital bedside and said, "We think it's a tumor, and most likely it's cancer."

The One I turned to in all of those heartbreaking situations was the same One I had cried out to as I hurried down the ship's stairs that day so long ago. The same One who gave me a thankful, joy-filled heart as I climbed back up those stairs was the same One who sustained me when grief was all I knew. He is the same One, now and forever.

*~ God, I trust you to support me on my journey whether I am filled with joy or emptied by grief. When my road takes hard turns, remind me that your love never ends. Amen.*

# Two Turtle Doves

THELMA WELLS

~

*We felt like we'd been sent to death row,*
*that it was all over for us. As it turned out, it was the*
*best thing that could have happened. Instead of trusting*
*in our own strength or wits to get out of it,*
*we were forced to trust God totally—not a bad idea*
*since he's the God who raises the dead!*
*(2 Corinthians 1:9 MSG)*

ONE BEAUTIFUL, SUNSHINY DAY I WENT TO my front door and was taken aback with the gorgeous basket of flowers being held by a smiling delivery man. I started to cry when I saw them because this was clearly a basket of love, not just the usual flower arrangement. The man's face was shining as bright as the sunshine glowing in the sky. He just beamed at me and said, "I'm so glad you like them." Then he briskly walked back to his white delivery van and drove off.

My friend Judy had sent the flowers to congratulate me on an award I had recently received. Immediately after reading her card attached to the flowers, I called Judy to thank her and to ask her where in the world she had found a florist that did that kind of endearing work. She told me this story . . .

"Thelma, that man was a bank officer for over thirty years.

He was recruited out of college and started as an officer in this bank without any experience or having to interview. He had given all of his working years to this institution. But in the fallout of bank failures, downsizing, outsourcing, and budget cutting, he was one of the first people to be asked to take a severance package. He had no choice but to leave with as much dignity as he could under the circumstances. This loss completely devastated him. He went into deep depression, tried to commit suicide, the whole nine yards.

"To make matters worse, the sizable profit sharing he received was deposited into a savings and loan that became the target of a lengthy lawsuit, and his money was tied up, without recourse, for years. He had no income, no money, no benefits. Life was tough!

"But through the haze of embarrassment, feelings of incompetence, inability to make ends meet, struggles with physical and emotional stability, and spiritual turmoil, there was a flicker of sunshine. His wife noticed that when he was working with the flowers they had planted in their backyard, he seemed calm. In fact, he appeared happy. The process of convincing him to go to a community college in Dallas and take a floral decorating course was arduous. But finally he consented. That turned out to be one of the best decisions of his life. There in the environment of flowers and the creativity of designing the arrangement of foliage, flower stems, and blossoms, this man found his calling in life. He regained his zest for living things and his zeal to live himself.

"When he first started making arrangements he didn't charge for them; he just gave them to his friends for their birthday, anniversary, or special occasion. But his appreciative friends convinced him to start his own business. He and his wife turned their garage into a florist workshop and called it 'Two Turtle Doves.'"

I asked Judy if I could call him. Our telephone conversation was life-changing for me. He confirmed the story that Judy had told me. But more than that, he told me how his life had meaning and completeness for the first time.

"Mrs. Wells," he told me, "I didn't realize that for thirty-three years I went to a job every day that I hated. I had nothing to compare it with. When you come right out of college into a job that gives you a great income and the luxuries of life, you tend to take it for granted and accept what it has to offer. I thought I would be there forever, enjoying the amenities of the country club, lavish vacations, big cars, a plush office, people serving me. I was complacent and submissive to the only career I had ever known. When I was forced to leave my position, I had no idea what we were going to do. But I'm so thankful for this experience now. I finally found out why I was born! I delivered your flowers to you. I love that! I get a chance to prepare the arrangements and deliver them to people and see their faces light up, see a sick person forget their pain for an instant, see a grieving person perk up with appreciation, and watch a bride celebrate her happy day. This means more to me than all the money in the world. You see, Mrs. Wells, my wife and I are no longer financially wealthy, but we're rich in things money can't buy. We live our lives through the happiness of others."

For this man, taking a totally unexpected fork in the road was difficult, but the rewards were equally unexpected and delightful. From the grateful florist I learned a big lesson for myself: God is our Provider; a job is a provision. When one job changes, another is waiting . . . and sometimes it's a whole new vocation that proves to be our highest calling.

With God as our Provider, any kind of loss need never be a total disaster. In fact, it can be the first step to a wonderful adventure.

*～ Great and loving Provider, renew the spirit of adventure in us so we can recognize the forks in our road as divine opportunities. Then give us the courage and ingenuity to travel down the new path with hopeful anticipation. Amen.*

# Laughter on the Line

## Barbara Johnson

~

*A man finds joy in giving an apt reply—*
*and how good is a timely word! (Proverbs 15:23)*

MY HEAD HAD TO BE SHAVED LAST YEAR
before my brain surgery, and for several weeks afterward I had
regular chemotherapy treatments, which ensured that any hair
that *thought* about growing back was quickly discouraged.
Then came several follow-up MRI scans. Before each one, the
receptionist at the radiology clinic would call to remind me of
my appointment. After telling me what time to be at the
clinic, she would add, "And remember: Don't wear deodorant
or use hair spray."

"Hair spray?" I'd say with a laugh. "To need hair spray, I'd
have to have HAIR!"

During one of my appointments I happened to be in the
waiting room as the receptionist was making her reminder
calls. I couldn't help overhearing when she called a man I
knew. "Remember," she told him, "don't wear deodorant or
use any hair spray." She paused a moment, listening and smiling, then she said good-bye and hung up the phone.

I had to laugh, thinking how ridiculous her reminder was.
I *knew* the man she had just called—and he was completely

bald! As gently as I could, I told the receptionist she was wasting her time, telling us chemo- and radiation-therapy patients we didn't need to wear hair spray.

"Oh, I know most of our patients have lost their hair," she said, smiling brightly. "I just say it hoping to give them a laugh. And usually it works."

*What a great idea,* I thought, smiling as I headed off for my MRI. The receptionist's easy way of spreading cheer reminded me of my friend who always leaves some kind of funny one-liner on her answering machine. Sometimes I call her just to hear her joke of the day. One day she mentioned a bumper sticker she'd seen recently. It said, "Honk if you love peace and quiet!" Another time she quipped, "Remember: In just two days, *tomorrow* will be *yesterday*."

Now, many of you know that I *love* one-liners; I collect them the way some people collect postage stamps or decorative spoons. Now, inspired by the radiology receptionist and my friend with the answering-machine funnies, I keep a stack of my favorite one-liners beside my phone to share whenever I make a call. For instance, I recently observed to my phone friends:

> The older you get, the tougher it is to lose weight,
> because by then your body and your fat are really
> good friends!

and . . .

> The sole purpose of a child's middle name is so he can tell
> when he's really in trouble.

Of course, not everyone laughs at such silliness. After all, we *choose* how we respond to the words we hear and the events that affect our everyday lives. There are probably cancer patients out there who are bitter about the hand life has dealt them, pessimistic about their futures, and resentful of those who seem more fortunate. So when they're standing there holding the telephone receiver to their hairless heads and the receptionist reminds them not to wear hair spray, they might roll their eyes and snort out a harsh reply. But what does that response get them? Only more bitterness. Not more hair.

On the other hand, think of the rewards we get if we choose to see the merry side of life. For one thing, we feel happier—and perhaps even healthier. Scientists are proving more and more links between laughter and health benefits. In fact, many hospitals now offer something akin to laughter therapy, providing videotapes of comedies and stand-up comedians for their patients to enjoy.

The next time the receptionist called to remind me of my MRI appointment, I was primed to take the high road to a belly laugh when she added, "And don't forget: no deodorant or hair spray."

Right after that, I called a Christian publishing company to ask about a bill I'd received by mistake. The man who answered my call said he didn't handle billing questions. Instead, he politely asked me to call a different number. He fumbled around on his desk, apparently looking for his phone list. "Here it is," he said, and he read off a number.

I called it and was automatically put on hold for a long time, listening to endless repetitions of songs like "Strangers in the Night" and "Who's That Girl?" *Strange music for a Christian organization,* I mused as I waited.

Finally, a woman came on the line. I laid out my question about the bill I'd erroneously received. "Uh, I think you have the wrong number," she said when I finished my explanation.

I read the number back to her, asking if I had misdialed.

"That's our number," she answered slowly. "But we don't do Christian publishing. We're a dating service for nudists."

"I've called a *dating* service for *nudists*?" I gasped.

"Yes ma'am. Sunshine Sweethearts."

I could hardly wait to call back the man at the publishing company. Redialing his number, it occurred to me that I had a choice to make: I could indignantly scold him for referring me to a company of dubious moral standing and icily demand that he give me the correct number. Or I could laugh about the mix-up and invite him to join me.

Do you have any doubt which choice I made? If so, just listen. You'll probably hear us laughing about it still.

~ *Dear Jesus, remind me daily that I have a choice about how I respond at every point along life's journey. Help me choose to share words that bring love, encouragement—and laughter—to all the lives I touch. Amen.*

# 'Cause Mama Said

## PATSY CLAIRMONT

~

*Do not forsake your mother's teaching. (Proverbs 1:8)*

HOW MANY TIMES HAVE YOU APPROACHED A
street crossing and wondered, *Now do I turn right or left?* More
times than I can count, I've looked like a bride doing the
hesitation step as I've lurched at an intersection, uncertain
which way to go.

Life choices can be disconcerting, which is why I'd love to
have well-lit billboards with luminescent arrows directing me.
Aw, who am I trying to kid? If my life were that structured, I'd
be hurdling the billboards in search of plan B.

That doesn't mean there haven't been times when I've
wished a telegram would fall from the heavens and end the
guesswork of some crossroads, for I have been known to ana-
lyze a decision to death, leaving myself befuddled. So I guess
I want selective help; I like to have choices.

When I was growing up, my mom didn't offer choices; she
had one way: hers. My sons would probably say the same
about me. Mom and I were fond of our own opinions, which
often put us at odds with each other. She was convinced when
I was a teenager that I never listened to any billboard advice

she gave me, but I absorbed far more than she thought. In fact, Mom's basic training still serves to direct my size-five feet.

## MAMA'S SIGNPOSTS

### *"Small Tasks Are Worthy of Great Efforts"*

After a basic housecleaning, Mom always fluffed pillows, tucked sheets, buffed silver, removed lint, arranged draperies, aligned pictures, and lit candles. She took time to fuss over the details that give a home those inviting, finishing touches.

To this day my eye delights in a well-tended setting. And, quite honestly, I love to include the same enhancements my mom did in my own home.

### *"Use Old Things in New Ways"*

Many a time I watched my mom root around in cupboards, closets, and basement corners searching for the right "something" to freshen the look of a room. She would also take a piece of furniture and place it in another room for a different purpose, giving a whole new look. She was inventive and creative.

Financially lean years made me grateful I could follow Mom's lead and change my home environment by spending only time and energy. I remember when my mother-in-law gave me an old family trunk, I immediately put it to use as a coffee table. She thought she was ridding herself of an eyesore (she kept it at the foot of her bed with a sheet over it), whereas I thought it was a valued treasure. Well, you know what they say: "One woman's trash . . ."

## "Wrap Gifts Carefully"

Mom believed that the way a gift was wrapped was a reflection of how important the person was to you. Ugh! Don't tell my mom, but I have handed gifts to important people in my life in the brown bags the presents came in. I'd slap a bow on the bag and was grateful I even remembered the special occasion. But when I've made the effort and designed the packaging, using my friend's or family member's favorite colors or interests, I've noticed the person always coos over it with pleasure.

One of the world's finest gift wrappers is Luci Swindoll. The presents she gives are works of art. One feels they should be photographed, to be mounted and hung at a later date, before proceeding with the grand opening. What a joy to be on her gift list.

## "A Well-Made Bed Sleeps Better"

When I was growing up, going to bed was always a pleasure. Mom often hung the sheets outside to catch the fragrance of the summer breezes. She would press the top sheet and the pillowcases until she had laid all the crumpled places straight. At bedtime she would turn back the bed and give the pillows one last fluffing.

My husband often teases me because I tuck our sheets in so firmly he needs a crowbar to get in bed. And pillow fluffing is a full-time occupation at my place, with rows of them covering half the bed. Turning back our bed requires a front loader just to de-pillow the spread.

### "Clean Houses Smell Good"

Not only was my mom a spit-shine cleaner, but she was also a fragrance bug. Not heavy smells, but fresh air, home cooking, lemon cleaners, and cedar closets. And even with her aerobic feats to keep our home tidy, she always smelled like a wild rose.

Keeping our home fragrant is difficult since both Les and I have sensitivities to many wonderful scents. We can do an air exchange by opening the windows for cross ventilation, and we seem to fare well with lemon-fragranced cleaning supplies and natural vanilla, but beyond that even our deodorant is unscented—boring! Of course, I prefer boring to heavily perfumed environments that make you feel as though you're wearing the air around you.

### "Dinner's Not Over Until Dessert"

This Mama billboard has far more to do with finishing what you start than it does with strawberry shortcake, although it is true we always had at least a dab of sweets to bring closure to a meal. Even when Mom hadn't baked or made a trip to the bakery, she would offer half a teaspoon of soft butter and two tablespoons of syrup, mixed together and dappled over a warm homemade biscuit. Yeah, Mom!

I love desserts, and it shows. So I often have to back off from the sweet tradition. Instead, I remind myself that my mom was a finisher of her tasks. Whatever she took on, she completed. I'm a little weak at this one. My tendency is to get bored with a task and fizzle, but because of Mom's example and the Lord's promise that he will be strong in our weakness, I have improved as a finisher over the years, and that has been a sweet touch to my adventure through life.

See, Mom, I was listening. And what you taught me often has been a helpful nudge in the right direction. Of course, the most important signposts you left me were the ones directed toward Jesus and his ways. I'm grateful you allowed him to change your life when you were in your late thirties. Otherwise, you could have been a taskmaster (me, too) instead of a tenacious teacher of truth. I watched your life, attitudes, and heart enlarge as you followed the Lord with the same passion and devotion you heaped on your family. I appreciate your going ahead and leaving me a clear path to follow. Thank you for showing me how simple attitudes and actions can enhance my journey every step of the way.

~ *Lord of my life, I celebrate the festive design of my days. It has been a pleasure unwrapping them. Thank you for your fragrant presence throughout the rooms of my life, as well as your faithful guidance. Remind me to take seriously and fervently, regardless of size, the task at hand, realizing I do it as unto you. In the sweet name of the Finisher of my faith, Jesus. Amen.*

# Jesus Will Repay

## LUCI SWINDOLL

~

*May your father and mother be glad;*
*may she who gave you birth rejoice! (Proverbs 23:25)*

IT HAPPENS ALMOST EVERY DAY. WHEN people understand that my brother is Chuck Swindoll—best-selling author, leading pastor, radio Bible teacher, and seminary president—the question always comes. When they know my only other sibling is Orville, who's spent his entire adult life as a well-known and exceedingly well-loved missionary in Latin America, I can be sure they are going to ask: "What was your mother *like?*" or "What did your mother *do?*"

To be honest, it's a question I've pondered and something I would love to know myself. Did my parents set out on a determined path to have their only three children go into public ministry? Were they perfect teachers and sublime models of our faith? Was my mother a saint? Were we brainwashed? Proselytized? Bribed?

I don't think so. As mothers go, mine was commendable, flawed, and a remarkable person. With no initial ambition to be a mother, her desire was to pursue art, a professional singing career, and a life of adventure. That all changed when, in rapid succession, she delivered three children who were "made in her image." We were, to borrow an old-fashioned term, a handful. We were energetic, inquisitive, imaginative, verbal, active, and utterly time-consuming. My mother found herself at a definite fork in the road—a place for which she had no training or preparation. What's a mother to do?

Rise to the challenge. I once asked Mother how she always knew what to do when we were children. Her answer was, "I didn't." Could o' fooled me. She always seemed to *know*. And she seemed to *do* everything well. The three of us have lived long enough to sing her praises and honor her memory.

I remember three things in particular that characterized my mother's life every day. First, she *read her Bible*. I can envision her now, sitting on the edge of her bed, holding the Bible with one hand and underlining verses with the other. She often memorized Scriptures and asked us to test her on them. She studied God's Word and applied it daily to her life.

Mother *prayed for us* faithfully. We were three strong-willed kids with wild fantasies, sibling rivalries, and minds of our own. We needed all the prayer we could get. Mother found verses that she "claimed" for us. She believed God would keep his word about providing and directing us into the path of righteousness. She encouraged us to pray and believe and leave the answers to the Lord.

And third, Mother *gave us to God*. I don't mean she sacrificed us on some imaginary altar; I mean she came to the conclusion that her three children were gifts to her and Daddy for the purpose of training and rearing, but ultimately, she let us go. She recognized we belonged to God and she consciously gave us to him . . . lock, stock, and barrel.

I have to say this, though, before we go too far: *None of this was easy.* By nature, my mother was moody, temperamental, artistic, and controlling. She wanted her way and she admitted that. But, somewhere in the course of God's bringing her to maturity he taught her that his way was better than hers, and she believed him. She realized he had put her in her life circumstances. He hadn't called her to be an artist, a musician, or an exotic adventurer. Her adventure was going to be as a mother, *our* mother. And he enabled her to live in ways that pleased him and were right for us.

But Mother had her hands full . . . just as you do, I'm sure. She was tested to the limit, and there were countless times she wanted to flat-out give up. But (and here's another characteristic of her high calling) . . . she never did. She hung in there when the going was tough, the cupboard was bare, and the purse was empty. She stood her ground for what she believed, and she trusted that God would come through. And he always did.

Mother used to sing all the time around the house—praise music, hymns, and patriotic songs. I recall one hymn in particular that was often on Mother's lips, "O Zion, Haste." Mother knew all three verses by heart, but it's the third that brings her most vividly to mind:

Give of thy sons to bear the message glorious;
Give of thy wealth to speed them on their way;
Pour out thy soul for them in prayer victorious;
And all thy spending Jesus will repay.

That is exactly what my mother did. She poured out her soul in prayer for her children, she supported us with her spirit of encouragement, and she gave us back to God to do whatever he wanted with us.

With all three of us now in Christian ministry I cannot help but wonder if this is the way Jesus repaid my mom for her years of believing, praying, and giving. I will never know this side of heaven how all this works, but I do know that when one is faithful to God's calling, he sees to it that there is reward and blessing in uncommon ways.

I believe my mother faced the same problems back then that mothers face today. And to make it through, she must have said to herself more than once: *God has called me!* And, when God calls, he enables. If Mother hadn't believed that, then how could she have ever gotten through life? If we don't believe it, then how can we?

We will never be able to successfully take care of life's problems on our own. But, that's the whole point: We don't have to. God will help us. As we come up for air, take him at his word, put one foot in front of the other, breathe deeply, and do the next thing, he somehow comes through with the goods. He shows up . . . and we make it.

~ *Thank you, Lord, for all the mothers who give their lives for their children. Honor them with your blessing, grace, and peace. Assure each one of us that when we do what we are called by you to do, there is great reward. Amen.*

# When the Going Gets Tough

THELMA WELLS

~

*The LORD is my strength and my song;*
*he has become my salvation. (Exodus 15:2)*

PERHAPS YOU READ BUMPER STICKERS ON
the backs of vehicles as I do. One day when I was broke,
bummed out, and disgusted, I was having a major pity party
while driving down the freeway. In front of me was a truck
with a bumper sticker that displayed in large letters, "Life is
tough, and then you die." Not what I wanted to hear that day.
No, the "adventure" of having only twenty-five cents in my
pocket, nothing in the bank, and no sweepstakes possibilities
in view was about to drive me to my wits' end.

My pity party got more raucous with every passing second.
Whimpering and gasping for breath, I noticed lights flashing
on an automobile dealership sign just ahead. I almost couldn't
believe my eyes when I got close enough to read: "Tough times
don't last. Tough people do!" This sign was flashing on the
watts of a whole different current. A second ago I was dying;
instantly after reading Dr. Robert Schuller's famous words, I'd
become a "tough" person who understood that "this, too, shall
pass." My pity party came to a screeching halt.

I learned a lot from that little drive. Life is full of experiences that challenge, confound, and concern us—and create circumstances that cause the road in front of us to take turns we don't anticipate or welcome. We get news we didn't want and can't send back by overnight mail. Family situations are strained. We feel as though even our best friends don't understand what we're going through. Life feels so tough sometimes that we wish we were dead. I know. I've been there.

But I've also been there for the resurrection moments. Just when I feel that I can't take one more second in the black hole of my own hope-starved soul, God shows up in ways I don't anticipate. I get "zapped" by a jolt of encouragement on the side of the road. I turn over a rock in the path and discover a treasure instead of more torment. I get to the bottom of the barrel and find out there's a way of escape. The bottom drops out and I land in the palm of God's hand.

> For God, who said, "Let light shine out of darkness," made his light shine in our hearts to give us the light of the knowledge of the glory of God in the face of Christ.
>
> But we have this treasure in jars of clay to show that this all-surpassing power is from God and not from us. We are hard pressed on every side, but not crushed; perplexed, but not in despair; persecuted, but not abandoned; struck down, but not destroyed. We always carry around in our body the death of Jesus, so that the life of Jesus may also be revealed in our body. (2 Corinthians 4:6–10)

If that's not a powerful description of what adventure is all about in the life of a believer, then I don't know what is. I don't naturally welcome being hard-pressed, perplexed, or persecuted any more than you do. But when the dark experiences of life come knocking at my door, I am promised that light will be provided in the midst of my bewilderment. And not just any light, but the glorious spiritual light that only the presence of Christ can give. When the going gets tough and I feel like death warmed over, in my very worst moment of misery the bright light and life of Jesus can be revealed. In the glow of his presence my whole attitude can shift instantaneously. A miracle!

I believe that's what I experienced when my road seemed so overwhelmingly rough and dark that day on the freeway. In one moment I was absolutely convinced that the message in front of me was true: "Life is tough, and then you die." No hope. No point. No adventure. But just up the road was a little fork on my right—a blinking, dazzling truth I'd completely forgotten as my pity party kicked into high gear: "Tough times don't last. Tough people do."

You are tough because the Spirit of God lives in you—and if anyone tells you otherwise, you want to meet them outside. Whether things are good or bad, happy or sad, difficult or easy, you're in the middle of a God-ordained adventure that changes day by day—sometimes second by second. You are never abandoned, never destroyed. When the going gets tough, the tough in Christ get going because *God* is faithful. Embracing an adventuresome life in spite of life's ups and downs requires a knowledge of God's ways, faith in his promises, a belief in his goodness and love, and a choice to live moment by moment under his grace.

Look up for a moment from whatever you're focused on and

notice what may be just beyond your sight. Keep moving forward, and you'll see a beacon of hope at the next fork in the road.

~ *Gracious God, thank you for not only putting up with our tantrums and shortsightedness, but for blessing us with unexpected reminders of your perfect timing and faithfulness. Help us to look up and see that you are truly with us every step of the way. Amen.*

# Part 3

~

## OFF THE
## BEATEN TRACK:

### LET CURIOSITY BE YOUR GUIDE

# One Surprise After Another

LUCI SWINDOLL

~

*He searches the sources of the rivers and*
*brings hidden things to light. (Job 28:11)*

SOME OF THE BEST ADVENTURES I'VE EVER HAD
were in out-of-the way places: down dusty roads, through the
backwoods, on trains or buses to unknown destinations. I've
often thought, *I'm glad God knows where I am, since I don't
have a clue.* And when I've taken time to go off the beaten
track in faraway lands I've always come home with the sweetest, most unusual stories and memories. I have journal entries
and pictures to prove it. "Yup! I was really there. That's me on
the back of that donkey, believe it or not. I was much younger
then . . . thin and cute!"

A couple of these wonderful excursions come to mind.

The first one happened in Greece when my friend Carla
and I went to Athens to see a Greek family I've known many
years and visited often. Right off the bat we decided to take a
side trip to somewhere in the country we'd never been before.
I had vacationed on a number of the popular Aegean islands
in the summertime, but here it was October, so Carla, Sophia
(my Greek friend), and I put a map on the floor in front of us,
closed our eyes, and pointed. Bingo! *That's where we're going on*

*vacation.* Since all of Greece is interesting and beautiful, we knew we wouldn't be disappointed no matter where we were headed.

Sophia's finger had pointed to Volos, a harbor/seaport town about five hours north of Athens. We grabbed our bags, a sack lunch for the journey, cameras, and journals and went to the bus station. As we bumped along on winding roads, we visited, snapped pictures, and snoozed. Finally arriving in Volos, we asked a taxi driver to take us to the most picturesque village he knew of. Before long we found ourselves in Milies, (*mill-yes*), a quaint, interesting place, nestled in the heart of the Pelion Mountains. None of us had been there (I'd never even *heard of* it), didn't know anyone, didn't have reservations, and had no idea if we'd even find a hotel or *pensioné* in which to stay. As the taxi pulled away, we might as well have been in Nowheresville.

Sophia scouted around, walked through the square and down a hill until she found a private residence that took in wayfarers like us who wanted bed and board for a few days. We were thrilled! The village itself was marvelous—flowers growing in pots on the front steps of little houses; an old church; a beautiful library (the oldest one in Greece); cats (ducking in and out of alleyways); cobblestone streets; and a clean, available, wonderful home that actually welcomed us with open arms.

"I like it here," I said to my pals. "Let's stay forever."

It turned out that the woman who owned the place was the most interesting aspect of the whole village. Her name was Despina—a single, attractive woman in her thirties who spoke five languages fluently, switching rapidly between them. She seemed to have been everywhere and done everything. I was mesmerized as she entertained us with one story after another. Day after day she was the troubadour and we were her captive audience. Each night we fell into bed long after midnight.

Despina loved classical music, literature, art, and crafts, and she wove comments about those subjects into fascinating tales. I even learned a very dear friend of hers was the costume designer for the Dallas Civic Opera, with which I had sung years before. He actually made my costume for *Medea* in 1958. Such a small world!

When we left Milies after four colorful, wonderful days, it was pouring down rain. Despina and her two dogs walked us to the square so we could hail a taxi. I remember glancing back at her through the window as we said good-bye and seeing a look of loneliness in her face, like she was waving a final farewell to three dear friends.

It is very probable I'll never see Despina again, but her life is imprinted on mine forever. I would have missed that entire chapter in my journey had I not taken that trip to a place I didn't know existed.

The second adventure was equally as unexpected. It happened on a Baltic cruise in Denmark. Since we don't like prescribed tours, Mary Graham (my traveling companion) and I disembarked the ship in Copenhagen with no plans for how we'd spend the day in port. Because it was Sunday, many things were closed so we set out to explore and see where it took us. We caught a shuttle into the city and while there Mary read about a museum in the home of Isak Dinesen, north of Copenhagen in a seaside town called Rungstedlund.

"Let's go," she said. "We don't have to be back on the ship until tonight . . . we've got time." All by ourselves in this strange, charming country, we hustled to the train station and bought our round-trip tickets. We had to sort of feel our way along, not knowing the language or the exact route—first on a train, then a bus, then on foot—to Dinesen's home.

Mary and I had so much fun! We spent an entire afternoon in that memorable place. We went all through the house and saw the room where Isak Dinesen wrote *Out of Africa*. We walked out to her grave under an enormous tree behind her home. We saw her library, her personal things, and even heard a lecture about her life, work, loves, and death. I bought a poster and had it framed. Each time I look at it now, I remember that delightful day in Denmark.

On board ship that evening, various passengers were complaining about having a boring or unpleasant day because nothing was open and the tours were so crowded. When people asked what we did, we were thrilled to tell them about our once-in-a-lifetime excursion just a few miles up the road.

Simply keeping our imaginations open and our curiosity in gear gives us a passport to adventure. Many times we feel like victims of circumstances beyond our control, but so often that's not true. When we become proactive and willing to take a few risks, the world opens its doors to us. And when we walk through those doors, we're rewarded with unique treasures.

Likewise, when we trust the Lord for interesting journeys in life, I'm confident he gives them to us gladly. Our task is to step out by faith into the unknown. God's task is to show us where beauty and mystery are hiding. He knows the way, and he delights in taking us there.

~ *Guide me today, O Great Jehovah. Lead me into a place of beauty, joy, worship, and discovery. Open my eyes and my soul to your enchanting surprises. In Jesus' name, amen.*

# "Hello . . . Stella?"

## MARILYN MEBERG

~

*Every good thing given and every
perfect gift is from above. (James 1:17 NASB)*

WHEN YOU LOOK INTO THE EYE OF AN ORANGE-
yellow egg yolk, what do you notice? If you were to ask me
that peculiar question about the egg on my plate, I'd say the
first thing I'd notice is whether the yolk was runny. Then I'd
notice if there is a light film of white over the yolk. If the yolk
is not too runny and not too hard with a light canopy of
white, the next thing I'd notice is the location of my fork.

The noted painter Peter Max had very different criteria for
evaluating an egg yolk. He says his first memory of color was
at the age of eighteen months when his mother placed an egg
in front of him. He was curious, fascinated, and thrilled. It
didn't matter if the yolk was soft or hard; he was excited by the
colors. With the passing of time he found the same colors and
more in his crayon box. His egg, crayon box, and ultimately
his oils, acrylics, dyes, pastels, and many other color media
have inspired an array of exuberant art known and appreciated
throughout the world.

What strikes me about that account is, even as a little fellow, Peter Max was naturally curious. That curiosity about

color potential led him on an expansive path of adventurous inquiry that ultimately produced beautiful art.

I think curiosity usually precedes the quest for adventure. My friend Pat Wenger is always curious about the inner workings of anything mechanical or technological. Because of this prowess we in the neighborhood call her "Mrs. Goodwrench." One morning she became curious about the inner workings of her master-bedroom toilet. It had a continual slight "run" for no efficient reason. (Actually, I suppose she was experiencing an element of annoyance in addition to her curiosity.) During a trip to a home improvement store she acquired the necessary tools for the task guaranteed to eliminate the "run." Buried to the waistband in her toilet, she exulted to me as I stood watching in the doorway, "How many middle-aged women do you know who can pull a toilet apart and fix it?"

I was about to shout, "None!" when somehow an ill-advised tap of the wrench led to a gush of water and a broken tank. I headed immediately to Starbucks for two Mocha Frappuccinos to go. What better solace could there be for a soaked carpet and a toilet that now "ran" with a vengeance.

Now, we don't have to be a world-renowned artist or a neighborhood toilet wizard in order to experience adventure. But if adventure is predicated upon curiosity, then I'd suggest we all take a few moments to determine what kinds of things arouse our curiosity. That may open up more possibilities for adventure than had ever occurred to us. The fun thing is that those adventures don't have to be on a grand scale, like art and plumbing.

My curiosity is consistently aroused by either my contemplation of people or my interaction with people. Since I see and talk to people every day, there is no end to the adventure potential. For example, last week the phone rang and I noted "unknown caller" on my ID screen. Normally, I don't pick up an unknown caller because more often than not it's a solicitor, but this time I did.

"Hello . . . Stella?" the caller inquired.

"No, this is Marilyn."

"Where's Stella at?"

"I don't know."

"She livin' at home anymore?"

"No, she isn't."

"Where is she, anyways?"

"Actually, Stella ran off with the produce manager at Albertson's and no one has heard from her in weeks." (I know, I know. I probably deserve your judgment, but sometimes I'm low on impulse control.)

"Well, I'll be . . . How is your other kids?"

After I told her I wasn't really proud of any of them, she commiserated, told me about her son Eldon, who was "a sweet boy but short on sense," and then concluded the conversation with, "Tell Stella her dog's ready."

Let me encourage you to check your curiosity gauge and then let it be your guide toward some unimaginable experiences. Some of our most memorable, fun, quirky adventures are off the beaten track. And they may be no bigger than those offered by an "unknown caller." Actually, I prefer those to egg yolks anyway.

*~ I thank you, Lord, for the gigantic gifts like salvation and your continual presence. I also thank you for the small treasures that you intend simply for my pleasure and amusement. I'm glad you created me with a natural curiosity so I can experience your vast range of "color" in life. Amen.*

# Experiments in Fun

LUCI SWINDOLL

~

*But now, Lord, what do I look for?*
*My hope is in you. (Psalm 39:7)*

ONE OF THE MOST INTERESTING BOOKS I OWN
is called *Country Women—A Handbook for the New Farmer*. I
bought it about twenty-five years ago, thinking I might want
to refer to it from time to time. This one volume is a college
education in itself. It tells you how to select and buy land, use
various tools, fight brush fires, prepare soil, and raise rabbits,
pigs, poultry, sheep, and goats. It gives advice on what to do
about garden pests, how to can and freeze vegetables, how to
roof the house, and what's involved in making your own
cheese (I love cheese). It even has drawings, photos, and
poetry. My kind of book!

Sometimes I have the feeling I'm the quintessential pioneer
gal who just happens to be living in the twenty-first century.
Ask my friends. They'll tell you. There's little about me that's
stylish, I don't like many new or fancy things, and I've been
known to give gifts made from trash. Put that all together and,
honey, it spells Country Woman.

Now don't get me wrong . . . there are some things I don't
gravitate toward—country music, for example, or poor gram-

mar or cowboy boots or "white trash cookin'." But I do believe I could live in the wilderness and do fine. I've often thought I'd be the winner on the *Survivor* reality TV show, given the chance to compete. Those folks have to be creative, intuitive, self-reliant, and not afraid to experiment. I can do that. Why, *experiment* is my middle name.

Even as I write this, I'm conducting an experiment in the kitchen—baking a loaf of bread in a flowerpot. They say it works, but I don't know yet. (And who is "they" anyway?) At the moment, I'm waiting for the dough to rise in the sunshine. Stay tuned. (First question: Is it supposed to rise *today*?)

I've also got an experiment going on my patio. Living in the desert, if you want to grow flowers, you almost have to have an automatic watering system to take over on the days you're not home. And since I'm out of town many days of the year, I've been working on that system to get it ready. I've punched holes in plastic saucers, run tubing through those holes to go from plant to plant, and am still awaiting the verdict. (Second question: Can water run uphill?)

A number of months ago I decided to make vegetable stock. For weeks, I diligently saved the tops of carrots, bottoms of asparagus, stems of parsley, leaves of broccoli, peelings of tomatoes, skins of onions and potatoes, and froze all that roughage. When I could no longer close the freezer door, I threw it all in a pot and cooked it with water for hours, straining and draining it until I got pure vegetable essence. I'm now ready to add this delicious, healthy ingredient to pasta, soup, or sauces. (Third question: Will twenty-eight bags of vegetable stock keep for several years?)

Oh, my. I just checked on the bread dough. It's rising. I'm so excited!

Perhaps the most experimental thing I ever did was giving a friend a haircut. Neither he nor I had any idea how it would turn out, but since he was broke, didn't mind living dangerously, and cared little about how he looked, he said, "Sure, Luci, go ahead. It'll grow back."

Oh, the fun we had! We still laugh about that wild little escapade. I insisted on cutting it in the yard, just in case it all got out of hand and flew into the soup or something. For obvious reasons, I didn't give my friend a mirror to keep up with where I was as I whacked and snipped. Occasionally he'd make a comment about feeling lighter or cooler, but it wasn't until it was all over that he asked the sixty-four-thousand-dollar question: Can people who aren't religious ascetics wear hair shirts?

Sure. Why not?

One final confession about being a country woman at heart: I sort of wish I owned a truck—maybe an old '56 Ford pickup. That'd be great. I could drive it down to the Farmer's Market for fresh produce and cut flowers, or I could haul shingles if I decided to put a new roof on the house. Pickups come in handy.

Life has so much fun in it. Little things can thrill us to pieces when we make curiosity our guide. Sometimes we miss the joy and excitement of living because we're so busy looking for something expensive or out of the ordinary to give us a rush. It doesn't occur to us that everyday experiences have built-in challenges and thrills. What's more familiar or ordinary than baking bread, watering plants, making stock, or getting a haircut? Yet, how often do we see these activities as adventures?

Experiment a little with a meal or a project. Try looking at it in a new and different way. The Lord gives us everything we need to cook up adventure. We don't have to leave home to find it. We don't need more money or time. We simply need to ask the Lord, "What do I look for?"—and he'll show us the fun right in front of us.

*Father, keep me from getting bogged down in the syndrome of needing more "stuff" to be happy. Show me that a curious outlook combined with trusting you starts the ball rolling for living fully right now. I want to learn to be happy with what I have, and to find simple delights all around me. I can't wait for the next experiment in fun! Amen.*

# "Now What?"

## THELMA WELLS

~

*Ask and it will be given to you; seek and you will find;*
*knock and the door will be opened to you. (Matthew 7:7)*

MY FOUR LITTLE GRANDDAUGHTERS STAYED
overnight last Friday and all day Saturday. Little girls ages six,
five, four, and two. (Am I crazy or stupid or what?) These wild
women in the making took me on as many adventures in that
short length of time as I've had all year. Their minds are working in overdrive all the time, and there are absolutely no lim-
its to what they will try.

Our time together started with questions. Grammy, can we
dance tonight? Grammy, what are we going to have to eat tonight?
Grammy, can we watch a movie tonight? Grammy, who else is
coming over tonight? Grammy, have you seen my new dance routine? Grammy, where were you when I called you last week?
Grammy, are you going to be in town for my birthday? The bar-
rage of questions was only the beginning. Not only did my little
live wires not run out of questions, they did not run out of adventures that kept their attention, even if it was for just a few minutes.

They turned flips and did cartwheels on my bed until my
head was spinning. (Papa was in another part of the house,
thank God.) They rolled marbles across the floor, on the table,

and under the furniture until I made them find every one of the shiny orbs and put them back in the vase of flowers from which they were confiscated. They built a mountain with chairs and plastic pieces of their picnic table, then imagined that a volcano was erupting and they were running for their lives. When I called out their names, as they instructed me to do, the volcano stopped erupting. They wrapped my large, warm, colorful lap blankets around them like evening dresses and pretended that they were going to a formal affair or were beauty queens in a pageant. They tried on all my fur hats, boas, high-heeled shoes, gloves, and other gaudy jewelry and made themselves look their Sunday best.

In the midst of all their imaginative and creative writing, drawing, dressing, and oratory, they inadvertently nearly destroyed the tidiness of my bedroom, their bedroom, my office, and my kitchen by spilling stuff, dropping stuff on the floor, and stringing their belongings from one end of the house to the other.

Does it sound like I'm complaining? Absolutely NOT! I'm simply pointing out that children are on an adventure minute by minute, day by day. We adults can learn something from them.

Their natural curiosity prompts them to ask a lot of questions. I've heard that the only dumb question is the one not asked. So why do adults ask so few questions? Perhaps we think everybody expects us to have all the answers, and we don't. So we stop asking questions, we stop learning and experimenting, and we short-circuit our own experience of adventure.

Most children are not concerned about how tidy things are around them. They love to try new things, stop in the middle, leave the pile of whatever they're playing with, and move on to whatever catches their eye and imagination next. They're constantly on the move. When we get older, we tend to get too caught up in keeping our lives and circumstances tidy; we stop having enough flexibility in our routine to stop and follow wherever our imagination leads. And as a result, we usually stop having fun. Who made up that dumb grown-up rule?

When I've allowed myself to just forget about routine and doing things in the usual ways, my mind seems to open up to fresh and innovative ideas. Adventures I would have missed if I'd kept things in order pop up in front of me like a jack-in-the-box. How fun!

I guess the clincher for my granddaughters was when they were relaxing in the bathtub. (The earlier dancing was part of the "wear them out so they can sleep" strategy.) After they finished splashing the water and chasing the bubbles, they asked enthusiastically, "Grammy, what are we going to do now?" They'd played, messed up, fed their faces, exercised their minds and bodies, even screamed at, hit, and mildly abused each other in their childlike way—and had run Grammy a little loony. *Now what?* Surely there has to be more to do than sleep! They never considered just calling it a day. Their curiosity about what new adventure might be awaiting them was limitless.

I can't count the number of times recently that women who were once real go-getters—intelligent, creative, and energetic—have said to me that they are just tired of life. They are bored with the humdrum of their daily routines and relationships. They see no way out.

I have two words for that kind of thinking. As the kids in

my neighborhood would say, "Chill out." You sound like you're overburdened, brain-dead, and on life support in your mind. What you need is a shock wave to jolt your natural curiosity so you can go see what's off the beaten track.

Do you remember those "dumb" questions I mentioned? Start asking them of yourself and those you respect. Start replacing the self-defeating tapes in your head with statements like, "I can." "I will." "I have a bright future." "I love life and the people in it." Jolt yourself out of your mental ruts by using the magical tool of *wonder*. "I wonder what I'm missing that I've been too busy to investigate." "I wonder how I could look at my situation in a whole new light." "I wonder what's over there—just around the next bend, off the beaten track. I think I'll go find out!"

Draw yourself a hot bubble bath tonight and splash around for a while. Thoroughly enjoy the moment. Then, with childlike anticipation, ask your heavenly Father, "Now what?" The answer might be, "Get yourself to bed, woman! You're whipped!" Or it might be something totally outside your routine, like "Go ye into the kitchen at midnight and create for thyself a sundae with every kind of dollop and sprinkle ye can find."

Take it from my granddaughters: You never know what you might be missing if you grow up too much and stop asking, "Now what?"

~ *God, please revive in us a childlike attitude so we will dream, ponder, wonder, and pursue the abundant life that surrounds us every moment. Open our minds and our eyes to the many little adventures that are ours if we but ask for them. Amen.*

# Missionaries of Mirth

## BARBARA JOHNSON

~

*We are therefore Christ's ambassadors, as though*
*God were making his appeal through us. (2 Corinthians 5:20)*

IF YOU THINK OF MISSIONARIES AS FEARLESS explorers who work in the jungles of Africa, Debbie Petersen will turn your assumptions upside down. Debbie is a beautiful single gal who works as a missionary in Miami. (You also may have seen her serving as emcee at the Women of Faith preconference events.)

Debbie is an urban missionary, and I am constantly amazed by the creative and clever ways she spreads the gospel to an incredible assortment of people. Whether she's joyfully handing out gospel booklets on the bustling sidewalks of South Beach, sharing a good word with the bag boy at her grocery store, or hosting a coffee for some of Miami's famous celebrities and leaders, she is always finding new ways to go off the beaten path and win souls for Christ. And whatever she's doing, she's smiling and laughing and reflecting the pure *joy* of being a child of God.

While I think of Debbie as being courageous and clever, she describes herself simply as being curious. She wants to know everything about the fascinating people she meets. That makes Debbie a great listener, and when she meets someone new she makes it her goal to find out that person's interests or background. Then she keeps an eye out for magazine or newspaper articles that might offer news or laughter. Or she finds just the right greeting card to brighten someone's day. Whatever she finds, she sticks it in a bright envelope, addresses it wildly in her big, bold handwriting, and sends it off with love and a prayer. Debbie often tells audiences this is her "mail ministry." And, she says, "I'm always quick to spell it out for everyone— m-a-i-l—so I'm not misunderstood." Sometimes, if the timing is right, she might tuck in a little Scripture verse, but overall her message is just one of caring and sharing God's love.

Many of us grew up thinking of missionaries as people who helped others. Now, after seeing the work Debbie does, I realize we *all* have the potential to be missionaries—to each other. We can be missionaries sharing God's love and encouragement, not just to our church friends, but to those people we meet "off the beaten path," as Debbie does when she's standing on those South Beach sidewalks, sharing a kind word, a smile, and a booklet.

Knowing Debbie and the work she does has changed my perspective on my own circle of friends. I now think of them as missionaries *to me*. I'm blessed to have these cherished people in my life who call frequently, send me funny cards, and let me know they are praying without ceasing. They may not think of themselves as missionaries, but to me they're nothing less, because they are living examples of God's love in action. Like Debbie, they've been led by curiosity and caring to listen, really listen, to me. And that listening has resulted in lots of heart-to-heart conversation—not to mention abundant laughter!

When my head had to be shaved for my brain-tumor surgery, my friends threw a "hat shower" for me, filling my closet shelves with all sorts of hats, scarves, and other head coverings. One friend even gave me a giant Afro wig that stands more than a foot high! Anytime I'm feeling down, I just pull on that ridiculous wig. The next thing I know, I'm standing in front of the mirror, laughing. It's an instant mood lifter.

Now, you might not think of an Afro wig as a typical gift you would receive from a *missionary.* But maybe you're not thinking outside the box, looking off the beaten track, or pushing the envelope in considering who missionaries are or what they're doing these days. Maybe you're not thinking of *yourself* as missionary material.

Think again!

~ *Oh, Lord, thank you for the missionaries of faith and hope you send to all the world—and for the missionaries of encouragement and mirth you send to me. Help me to recognize them when they appear, and reveal to me creative ways I can return the joy. Amen.*

# And the Question Is . . . ?

## THELMA WELLS

~

*What do you think about the Christ?*
*Whose son is he? (Matthew 22:42)*

THE ADVENTURE OF EFFECTIVE COMMUNI-
cation is a real trip! The journey includes rituals, misunder-
standings, and clever responses. One ritual we engage in
almost every day of our lives can express genuine concern for
people or blatant indifference. Listen to this conversation (if
you can call it that):

"Hello. How are you?"

"Fine. How are you?"

"Fine. Thank you."

Okay, what's up wid dat? Two questions that may or may
not mean anything to the people involved. Usually this mind-
less exchange is just a way to say "Hello."

What happens when the ritual is challenged?

"Hello. How are you?"

"How much time do you have for me to tell you?"

I've said that just to see the reaction of the other person.
Most of the time people respond with a smile or laugh. That's
what people do when they don't know exactly what to say.

Sometimes they look at me as if I'm crazy. I guess they caught on that I might be a little off.

I heard this ritual proceed this way the other day:

"Hello. How are you?"

"I don't feel good today. I'm sick."

"Oh, that's good."

The person who asked the banal question wasn't even listening to the answer! She was off on another adventure that had absolutely nothing to do with the person she was talking to.

So, the question is, how effective is this ritual? It provides an avenue to be polite without really getting involved.

The art of effective communication has never been so powerfully demonstrated by any person as by one Man. People would ask him questions or make statements to him either out of genuine curiosity, or to try to trick him. He was always listening acutely to whoever was engaging him, and often his responses would end with a question or two of his own.

Jesus was speaking in a crowded house, and his mother and brother were standing outside wanting to talk to him. When someone told him they were there, he remarked, "Who is my mother, and who are my brothers?" (Matthew 12:48). Can you imagine how that confounded his listeners? *What is he talking about . . . who is his mother . . . who are his brothers? He talks like he's off his rocker.*

But Jesus' questions are always cleverly designed to lead us to a better understanding of him and ourselves. "Pointing to his disciples, he said, 'Here are my mother and my brothers. For whoever does the will of my Father in heaven is my brother and sister and mother'" (Matthew 12:49–50).

When Jesus and his disciples were nearly shipwrecked while Jesus was asleep in the bottom of the boat, his frightened and frantic friends abruptly woke him, asking, "Teacher, don't you care if we drown?" (Mark 4:38). I can just imagine Jesus gently waking up to their shouts, reaching out his hand and saying to the wind and waves, "Quiet! Be still." In the immediate calm that followed, he turned to his amazed disciples and asked them two questions: "Why are you so afraid? Do you still have no faith?" (Mark 4:40).

In the midst of people's often meaningless communication rituals, and in spite of their misunderstanding and misinterpreting, Jesus consistently gave wise and clever responses that were designed to both uproot people's erroneous assumptions and widen the scope of their vision. By asking thought-provoking and penetrating questions, he aroused people's curiosity—and sometimes their ire. He was a master communicator, and he is our model.

So the question is, When you interact with others, will you choose the dull, predictable route, or will you venture beyond the routine to take a conversation off the beaten track? Most important, will you stay conscious of and connected with the Source of the most clever and important question ever asked of us, "Who do you say I am?" (Mark 8:29). Will you answer his question with the same confident passion that Peter had? "You are the Christ." If you answer that question with that statement, you can experience absolute liberation on your journey through life. You need never be stuck in ritual or routine because the Savior himself is with you, giving you courage and freedom to explore and experiment, risk and love.

So do it! Fire up your curiosity and ask someone a question that will get the creative sparks flying. Realize that because you have the Holy Spirit within you, you can become a master communicator.

~ *Jesus, as we communicate with other people, may your Spirit blaze within us. Thank you for showing us how to interact in creative and life-transforming ways. What an adventure! Amen.*

# A Novel Idea

LUCI SWINDOLL

~

*Whatever you have learned or received or heard from me,*
*or seen in me—put it into practice. (Philippians 4:9)*

THERE'S AN IDEA AFOOT THAT'S FANTASTIC. IT'S the nation's hottest intellectual trend, called "One Book, One City."

Starting in Seattle, moving next to Los Angeles, and then taking Chicago by storm, various city leaders decided to do something that would bring together folks of different backgrounds. With such ethnic, educational, professional, and financial diversity that characterize our cities today, they looked for a way to combat one of the greatest dilemmas in modern life—loneliness. And they found it—in communal reading, of all things. Everybody was invited to read the same book at the same time and talk about it among themselves. This "City-Reads-a-Book" movement has sparked a thirst for conversation.

Take Chicago, for example. Mayor Richard Daley asked all three million citizens to read Harper Lee's *To Kill a Mockingbird*, a book about a white lawyer who defends a black man accused of rape in a Southern town in the 1930s. The response to Mayor Daley's request was electric. In seven weeks more than sixty-five hundred copies of Lee's classic were checked out of public libraries; the Chicago Bar Association held a mock trial (in costume) of the courtroom drama depicted in the novel; and there was a marathon weekend showing of the old movie starring Gregory Peck.

People began to notice that on the bus, in the bar, at the bank . . . everywhere . . . this book was the hottest topic of conversation. The city even published a resource guide for teachers and distributed lapel pins that asked, "Are you reading *Mockingbird*?" The library held book discussions, and anybody who participated got free Starbucks coffee and pastries. *Everybody* wanted in on the fun. They wanted to be part of an enriching project. *Mockingbird* became "cool"! As one guy said in a *Los Angeles Times* article I read, "There was a nice feeling of belonging to something."

There's the key: the "feeling of belonging." In that little statement there's a whole world of adventure—the adventure of togetherness and connectedness. We all want to belong. We want to feel cared about, included, considered, and valued. We want to be asked, "What do *you* think?" And this simple reading project started the ball rolling on that. What a novel idea!

A few years ago I was reading that great epic polar adventure, *Endurance*. It's the story of an expedition to the Antarctic and the incredible rescue that took place after the ship sank. Threaded throughout the book is an amazing account of courage, self-sacrifice, and leadership during the two years the captain and crew were in life-threatening conditions. I eagerly devoured every page.

And . . . on four different occasions in airports when I was either holding the book or reading it, people talked to me about it. I might as well have been wearing a lapel pin that asked, "Are you reading *Endurance*?" Each time the person asked if I liked it and why, then went on to tell me what *she* liked about it. For a few moments we were members of the "*Endurance* Club." I didn't know these people, had never laid eyes on them, but because we were reading the same book, we were conversing beyond the superficial "How ya doin'?" interaction.

After the atrocities of September 11, 2001, the whole nation—dare I say the whole world—started talking to each other. We were bound together by a cause that was no longer superficial or solitary. We needed each other.

And isn't that what we've known all along? When Jesus walked on this earth, he found meaningful ways to fellowship with others. He visited the homes of his friends, and ate there. They told stories and talked about the most important things in life together. He met people in the marketplace and talked with them. He conversed with others along the way as he went about doing the work of his Father. He spent more time in groups than alone. He loved his disciples and devoted friends, and he engaged in activity with the masses. He showed up at baptisms, funerals, weddings, and picnics. Jesus knew what it meant to be bound together with others. He referred to the church as his own body; that's how connected he was to humanity and how he intends us to be.

It doesn't surprise me that two thousand years later men and women like finding significant ways to connect. I remember reading the story a few years ago about the founder of Starbucks Coffee, Howard Schultz. His concept was to provide a place where people could come together and enjoy connecting—over coffee. I've noticed that the latest trend in many bookstores is similar. Stores used to just sell books; now the more popular ones throw in a coffee bar and overstuffed chairs and sofas— places for community. Whether it's reading a book, sharing a latte, or meeting anywhere for anything, we are created for connectedness.

The idea to read the same book at the same time may be novel and new to those who initiated the program, but the motive behind it is a very old notion to those who follow Christ. We were created with relationships in mind. We are designed to relate significantly to the Father and his Son through the Holy Spirit. And that same Spirit enables us to relate to one another.

The apostle Paul exhorted the early Christians, "Let us not give up meeting together, as some are in the habit of doing, but let us encourage one another" (Hebrews 10:25). So . . . let's get together. What shall we read?

~ *Heavenly Father, I want to put into practice today what your Son so beautifully exemplified while he lived on Earth. Arouse my curiosity and caring about other people so I will naturally ask questions and reach out to them with a genuine desire to connect. May I touch every person I encounter with your Spirit and love. Amen.*

# Fire and Lightning

PATSY CLAIRMONT

~

*There the angel of the LORD appeared to*
*him in flames of fire from within a bush. (Exodus 3:2)*

MOSES WAS TENDING HIS SHEEP WHEN A
certain sight nabbed his curiosity. A bush was encompassed in
flames. Since Moses had lived in the scorching desert some
forty years, I doubt that a burning bush was a rarity, but what
snagged Moses' interest was that the bush, while afire, was not
consumed. "So Moses thought, 'I will go over and see this
strange sight—why the bush does not burn up'" (Exodus 3:3).

Picture a lilac bush or an evergreen shrub engulfed in
flames, yet every leaf, every needle, every bud is unaffected by
the incinerating heat. No wonder Moses approached to see
how this could be.

The eighteenth-century author Samuel Johnson said, "A
generous and elevated mind is distinguished by nothing more
certainly than an eminent degree of curiosity."

Curiosity keeps inventions circulating the globe, allows
children's minds to grow, ignites creativity and progress, pre-
vents human stagnation, and keeps adventure as close as our
fingertips. Curiosity is infused with dynamics that challenge
us to investigate life.

The naturalist John Muir, while with friends at a mountain cabin, decided to investigate his surroundings. You'll never guess what stirred his interest. Okay, okay, I'll tell you. A wild storm rattled their cabin's rafters and ignited John's desire to find out what a storm's fury really felt like. So he braved the winds alone, at night, shimmied up a tall fir, and rode out the storm. Wow! Crazy? Perhaps. Brave? Well, *I* think so.

You see, as an agoraphobic throughout my twenties, I struggled with exaggerated fears. One of them was the fear of storms. I just knew every time a shutter rattled, a cloud appeared, or thunder rumbled in the heavens my life was over. I listened to twenty weather reports throughout the day—and that was during sunny forecasts. I was a walking, talking storm warning, a forecaster of doom. When a true storm would hit, I could be found in tears, running from window to window, or cowering under a table, or huddled in the basement, but most certainly popping tranquilizers.

Today I find storms exhilarating. Well, I'd prefer not to fly in them (or dangle from the tiptop of a fir tree), but otherwise I love the exquisite beauty and power they produce. And sometimes, when on a cross-country flight, I have witnessed lightning storms in the distance that created breathtaking aerial night views. I'm glad I didn't miss that perspective of the heavens declaring the glory of God and the skies proclaiming the work of his hands (see Psalm 19:1).

So many wondrous things happen during a lively storm that stir fascination. Many of the homes I've lived in were surrounded by trees, which would shake their heads vigorously during winds and rain, ridding themselves of dead branches, unwanted guests, and old fruit. And if you've ever walked a beach after a tempestuous storm, you know the swelling sea has taken the opportunity to unload shards of glass, drifts of wood, and eclectic debris.

I guess that's a storm's purpose—to cull weakness, deepen roots, purify, and promote growth, whether in a forest, an ocean, a nation, or an individual. And while it's blustery during the storm, peace—blessed peace—often follows.

Gradually, I've learned to face my fear of storms, physical and personal, by trusting God's plan in them, which has heightened my inquisitiveness toward life in general. I believe that as our curiosity and trust grow greater than our fears, we will have the courage to approach even a burning bush.

> Earth's crammed with heaven,
> And every common bush afire with God;
> But only he who sees, takes off his shoes;
> The rest sit round it, and pluck blackberries,
> And daub their natural faces unaware.
> —Elizabeth Barrett Browning

*Dear Lord, you have given us a curious world to explore. May we not hesitate to investigate even its fury. Guide us through lightning and thunder with a sense of adventure. May we witness your illuminating presence and aerial views in our darkest hours. Baptize our curiosity with your holy fire, that we might become your burning bush in someone's desert. Amen.*

# Panic on the Peak

## Thelma Wells

~

*Trust in the LORD with all your heart and
lean not on your own understanding. (Proverbs 3:5)*

DO YOU KNOW SOMEONE WHO LIKES TO CLIMB
mountains? My only question is, *Why?*

It has never made sense to me to put on all those heavy
clothes, strap on a backpack, haul water, wear high-top boots
with soles that look like tire treads, cover your head like a
mummy, wear glasses that you can hardly see through, and
trudge up some pile of dirt and rocks to see nothing but the
same dirt you saw on your way up. To me, that's a waste of
precious energy and unrecoverable time.

Obviously, I don't mountain-climb and I don't watch other
people mountain-climb. But when I hear climbers talk about
how adventuresome and exhilarating their hobby is, what a
rush and thrill they feel as they're climbing—especially when
they get to the summit—their enthusiasm does cause my eye-
brows to rise. Actually, I'm happy for them and glad it's not me.

You'll never catch me going up the rough side of a mountain because I don't like to wear that many clothes. The highest incline I tackle is the one on my treadmill, and it's set
barely above zero. If I were to climb a real mountain, I would

not be able to look down when I got to a pinnacle because I get dizzy looking down from a two-step kitchen ladder.

My daughter Vikki, on the other hand, has had her share of mountain-climbing adventures. She told me the story of climbing a mountain when she visited Japan. With some time to spare, she seized the opportunity to climb this mountain all alone. That's not unusual for my oldest daughter; she accomplishes many of her feats alone with God. All was going well as she made her way up the mountain path. Nearing the top, she came across a caution sign that advised, "Don't go beyond this point." Naturally she thought, *I wonder what's beyond this point. I'll just see. Surely they don't mean this.* So, Miss Curiosity-Killed-the-Cat continued past the warning sign. Walking happily along she thought, *Why did they have that sign there anyway? Everything's fine up here.*

As the afternoon light began to fade she looked around to get her bearings before starting her descent. Suddenly nothing looked familiar. She couldn't be sure which path led safely down the mountain. She began to feel a little woozy because of the high altitude. Fear began to grip her. She didn't know whether to climb straight down from where she was or to keep trying to find the trail she had followed coming up. You see, after she passed the warning sign she decided to take a slight tour around the summit. (As her mother, I think that is sooo stupid. But what do I know? I wasn't even there.)

Panic set in. Tears began to stream down her face. She began to hurry down the mountain from where she was, praying that she would get to the bottom before darkness enveloped her. That's right: "praying." She finally realized that she needed divine guidance to get back to safety. *Duh.* She began to beg God to help her. She asked God to pardon her for not asking for his wisdom and guidance *before* she began the climb. She asked God to forgive her for not paying attention to the warning sign. She asked God to help her not throw up!

Finally, as she scrambled down the mountainside, she started noticing some familiar landmarks. She started praising God and mentally spanking herself for going it alone, throwing caution to the wind, staying on the mountain longer than she should have . . . for being foolish. When she reached level ground, she discovered that she'd landed exactly where she'd started. The tears of fear on the summit became tears of thanksgiving as she stood secure at the base. God had brought her out victorious one more time.

That's the way it is for most of us. We try to go it alone without consulting the Master of our journey for instructions and directions. We wear heavy baggage of determination, commitment, control, tenacity—all of which are necessary for the trip, but do us little good unless we have the hand of God securing us. As we climb the situations of life, we, too, often disregard the caution signs because our curiosity outweighs our good judgment.

The wonder of it all is that when we can't see our way down or out, we can always renew our reliance on God and he will not only show us the way back, but he will also forgive us for going astray. Curiosity is a delightful and challenging attribute necessary to a life of adventure. But wouldn't our escapades be so much easier and more fun if we would consult the Master before we tackle the highlands that beckon us?

*⁓Master of the mountains of life, what a relief it is to know that whether we ask for your help before we forge ahead, or wait until we can't see our way, you are always there with your sustaining hand. Thank you for the invigorating quality of curiosity that you've created within us. Remind us to enjoy it wisely. Amen.*

# Walking on All Twos

MARILYN MEBERG

~

*Hold fast to Him. (Deuteronomy 11:22 NASB)*

WALKING THE LABYRINTH IS A CENTURIES-OLD tradition that is being resurrected and touted as a modern refuge, a place for spiritual contentment. It sounds like anything but a refuge to me, but see what you think.

Just in case you're rusty on the labyrinth, it is a rigidly designed path, usually made up of semicircles that ultimately lead to the physical center of the structure. Supposedly, the lure of the labyrinth is that it has no dead ends. Some believe that the one-way path leading to the center and back out again is a perfect place for prayer, relaxation, and contemplation. If you walk the path and persist, not only are there no dead ends, but you can't get lost and you'll eventually reach your goal.

So what do you think? Going in circles makes me nauseous—not contemplative and certainly not relaxed. Am I missing something?

I'm pretty certain I won't become a labyrinth walker, but I think I fear becoming a labyrinth-thinker—one who would choose a path in life that is predictable and assured. The end of the path would be utterly recognizable because it would not vary in appearance from the beginning. Now how dull is that?

If I fall into the category of a labyrinth thinker I'll become a person who is stifling, boring, and resistant to trying something new because I can't know its precise outcome. That also means I'd rarely know adventure.

My fear of the unknown could become an obstacle to going off the beaten track if I let it, because I like a certain amount of structure and predictability. I like my morning English breakfast tea, which must be brewed (no bags—I claim I can taste the paper), and I'm irritated if the phone rings too early because it interrupts my reading of the newspaper. (I know it would sound more spiritual and certainly boost my image if I said I had my devotions before I read the paper, but I don't. I love it that God does not mind.) So, as I contemplate the possible lure of labyrinth thinking, I remind myself I have a choice. By simply being aware of the possibility of getting into a rut, I can choose to resist that outcome by keeping my curiosity and open-mindedness intact.

In my desire to choose the more adventuresome path, I've recently been inspired by a dog named Daisy—a two-year-old beagle who can walk on her front legs. With her back legs stretching straight up into the air, she can go down stairs, walk through the house, and entertain at family barbecues. The show-off potential of Daisy's front-paws-only walk is endless.

Daisy came to realize her uniqueness when her adolescent owner, Nicole, decided to dress Daisy in doll clothes. After a pair of baby booties were slipped on the beagle's back paws, she suddenly began walking on her front ones. Since Daisy performs "her trick" only when she's wearing booties, a possible assumption is she doesn't want to get her booties dirty by walking on them. Whatever is in Daisy's puppy brain, I love her innovative and enthusiastic alternative to the dog trot. She apparently has no concern with its uncertain outcome.

We all have a natural need for order and structure in our daily living. Without it our lives can feel out of control and even chaotic. God is a God of order, and because we bear his imprint, we, too, need order. However, isn't it interesting that God cannot be put in a box; we can't figure out his reasoning or come anywhere near to fully knowing why he works in the ways he does. To walk with him on a path where we cannot see the end from the beginning requires total trust. He promises a light for our path, but that light does not shine past the current footprint.

How do I feel about that? More often than not, I want a broader beam.

But to see more precisely where I'm going and why requires less faith. Less faith leads to a diminished walk with the Father characterized by even less vitality. I don't want that. I want a vibrant, exuberant, trusting relationship with God. I also want a spirited, creative, confident response to the life he has given me on Earth. I'm with Daisy on that one.

~ *Lord, this life is an adventure. Unlike the labyrinth, we have no idea what's ahead of us. May we trust you for the path you've put us on, and may we never forget that only your love makes our destination secure. Amen.*

# Part 4

~

## OUT ON A LIMB:

### RISK A LITTLE . . . OR A LOT

# "It Came to Pass . . ."

## BARBARA JOHNSON

~

*The disciples went and woke him, saying,*
*"Lord, save us! We're going to drown!" . . .*
*Then he got up and rebuked the winds and the waves,*
*and it was completely calm. (Matthew 8:25–26)*

COME ON. IT'LL BE AN ADVENTURE," BILL SAID, coaxing me into agreeing to a ten-day cruise to Hawaii. I was reluctant to go. After nearly a year of coping with cancer and the side effects of chemotherapy, I was finally feeling almost well again. But I hadn't ventured far from home in all those months, and I wasn't sure I was ready for a long, transoceanic voyage.

Still, I wanted to do something to please Bill. For years, we had enjoyed traveling all over the country together, and he loved visiting new places. During my treatment and recovery from a malignant brain tumor, he had rarely left me alone for more than two hours at a time. My doctor had even told me it was Bill's diligence in helping me follow the chemotherapy protocol so precisely that had led to my current state of health. There had been some days when I'd had to take a total of eighty pills throughout each twenty-four-hour period—a requirement that would have been beyond my patience and persistence if I'd been left on my own. But Bill had dutifully sorted out the medications into a muffin tin, set his wrist-watch to beep whenever it was time for another dose, and then made sure I swallowed each and every pill at exactly the right time. He deserved a reward, so I agreed to the cruise, trying to hide my misgivings.

To put it bluntly, the trip was a disaster.

Before we even got on the boat, I tripped over a board on the walkway, fell down, and broke my front tooth! The thought of compulsively running my tongue over that jagged edge for ten days nearly sent me into a panic, but remembering my goal of letting Bill have a good time, I assured him I would be fine—even if I did resemble one of the cast members on the old hillbilly show *Hee Haw*!

We settled into our cozy stateroom and prepared for ten laid-back days of relaxation as the ship left the pier and headed west. Before we were out of the harbor, however, I felt the tiniest little disturbance in my stomach. By the time we sailed into the open waters of the Pacific, huge waves were heaving the ship like an enormous rocking horse—and I was doing some heaving of my own! The good news was, I was so miserably seasick it completely distracted me from worrying about my broken tooth for the rest of the day!

The bad weather continued, and I was stuck in my stateroom, seasick for three long days as the ocean heaved around us. There were times during that period when I looked back fondly on the side effects I'd suffered from the chemotherapy treatments, thinking that the chemo nausea had really been quite pleasant, in retrospect. While Bill, reminiscing about his seagoing days in the navy, was strolling the decks and breathing in the fresh air, I was curled up in my bed, running my tongue over the stub of my tooth and praying God would give me strength to stagger to the ship's railing so I could throw myself overboard.

When we finally disembarked in Honolulu, I was so glad to be back on dry land that I almost followed the pope's practice of kneeling to kiss the ground. Then, after a much-too-brief stay, we were crammed back onto the ship, this time bound for the port of Hilo. There, the seas were too rough for us to land, so I longingly watched out the window as the ship made a gradual turn away from the big island and headed back toward open sea. Although my seasickness finally diminished, I was still unable to stand the sight or smell of cooked food, which, of course, is a highlight of ocean cruises. So I spent most of the return trip in my stateroom, reading and nibbling on crackers and peanut butter.

In all my days, I've *never* been so glad to get home as I was when that trip ended.

For the first few days after we got back, I fondly referred to our trip as "the cruise to hell and back." Then the dentist fixed my broken tooth, and gradually the terrible memories softened into funny stories I shared with friends.

Now, as I think back on my experience, I see parallels between the Christian life and being seasick. Jesus never promised us smooth sailing through life, but he did promise us a glorious homecoming. There were times, while I was parked in the bathroom, that I was so sick I thought I could not go on. I wanted to die. Similarly, there have been times in my life when I've been so miserable and heartbroken that I've prayed, "Dear God, please take me *now!* I cannot endure one more moment, one more breath."

And yet, even when I was sickest on that ship, I knew the illness was only temporary. As awful as it is, seasickness doesn't kill people (although they sometimes wish it would!). In the same way, troubles that beset my earthly life are also temporary. When hard times hit, I remind myself of the wonderful phrase that appears 457 times in the King James Version of the Bible: "It came to pass." And I cling to the lifeline of God's Word, promising me that at the end of this earthly voyage, I'll have the most glorious homecoming imaginable.

~ *Every day I turn to you, Lord, and ask you to save me again. And every day in every way you do. I praise you that, because you are always with me, I can risk unsettling voyages and live to tell! Amen.*

# Branching Out

## PATSY CLAIRMONT

~

*[Love] . . . always trusts, always hopes,*
*always perseveres. (1 Corinthians 13:7)*

I GLANCED OUT MY LIVING-ROOM WINDOW
only to be startled by someone looking back at me. It was a ban-
dit. I knew because she wore a mask. But that covering didn't
hide her identity; I could still tell she was a raccoon—a very
young raccoon with a big problem. Hanging on for dear life, eyes
like saucers, she was stranded out on a limb in my cherry tree.

Codependent me wanted to shinny up the tree and rescue
this furry thief who had been swiping my fruit. Even though
she and her family had diminished my cherry supply, I held no
grudge. Her downcast whiskers and pitiful whine made my
heart hurt. Poor baby.

"Les, come help," I called to my husband.

Les arrived and quickly scoped out the situation. "Oh,
don't worry, Patsy. Mama will be back to guide her home."

"But, Les, she's so little, so afraid, and she's dangling rather
precariously."

"Don't worry. She won't fall. She was designed to hang on
until help arrives."

"Maybe we're the help," I suggested.

"Okay, I'll get the ladder, and you can bring her down. You've had your rabies shots, haven't you?"

"Look at her sweet face; she couldn't possibly have rabies. Could she?"

Les wagged his head and suggested that I not go out on a limb myself by interfering.

In past days we had seen the raccoon family milling about the property. Mrs. Raccoon had five youngsters, so it's possible she hadn't yet taken a head count and didn't realize little sister was still up a tree. A short time later I looked out my window to find tiny saucer-eyes gone. I'm certain Mama arrived home and did a roll call, only to discover that she needed to scamper back and retrieve her little one.

Going out on a limb is precarious at best. Even as we do it, we have an inkling that this is risky. The fall could be harmful; yet sometimes, relationally, the limb is just the place to be.

Recently, I watched a television program where people were sent out in pairs to reach a certain faraway location. One of the teams was a mom and a daughter who were not only joining in the race for the adventure of it but also to deepen their relationship. It turned out they had missed important years of bonding. The parents had divorced, and the dad had raised the girl. So Mom and daughter had decided to go out on a limb and risk the trip. They knew they would be asked to work as a team and that they would have to do things outside their comfort zones.

Sure enough, one of the first assignments was to rappel down a mountainside. The drop was about six hundred feet. Eek! Fighting back sheer terror, the mom cinched up and inched down the craggy incline. And I do mean "inched."

Ever so cautiously she made it to the bottom, only to have to rush off to their next destination. (I can only imagine how wobbly Mom's legs must have been.)

Unfortunately, when they arrived at the first rendezvous, the mother-daughter team was eliminated from the rest of the contest. Mom's rappelling attempts were just too slow. She was crestfallen, realizing their elimination was her fault. The daughter, while disappointed, reassured her mom that she was proud of her efforts. Their exchange was heartwarming.

What a risky relational move for that pair. Both mother and daughter had something to lose and something to gain. It's difficult to work on relationships privately, much less in front of the world. But perhaps they found it worth the world to gain each other's respect, improve their friendship, deepen their familial bond, and branch out to experience new aspects of their relationship.

Can you think of at least one relationship in your life that needs shoring up? One that has been strained by misunderstanding, distance, or lack of involvement? What are you willing to risk to make changes?

~ *Lord, you not only were willing to go out on a limb, but you surrendered your life on a tree so that the world might know of your love. Give us the same heart to love regardless of the risk of rejection, neglect, or misunderstanding. Thank you that we have been designed, when we're out on a limb, to hold on until help arrives. The truth is, Lord, some of the best views we have of you are when we are vulnerable and trusting that you'll rescue us. Amen.*

# "I'm Not Okay with This"

### SHEILA WALSH

~

*An honest answer is like a kiss on the lips. (Proverbs 24:26)*

ONE OF THE HALLMARKS OF THE CONTINUING
message of Women of Faith is honesty. It's tempting in the
Christian community to dress up our lives and make it seem as if
we've always made good choices and inspiring decisions, but that
would not be true or real. We are committed as a team to share
how Christ has transformed us in the broken places of our lives.

I discovered some time ago that my brokenness is a far
greater bridge to others than my apparent wholeness ever was.
Our broken places allow the light and grace of Christ to shine
through. When Barbara speaks about her harsh reaction to
discovering that her son was involved in a homosexual relationship and then goes on to describe their ultimate reconcili-
ation, it gives other women who have reacted badly hope and
healing. When Patsy talks about the fear that gripped her life
and held her hostage within the four walls of her home, those
who struggle with that terror feel as if they are not alone. Anytime I mention my struggle with clinical depression, I am
amazed by the number of women who tell me that they suffer, too, and have never told another living soul apart from
their doctors—if they've even been brave enough to seek help.

Any specific situation that is shared from the stage at Women of Faith conferences carries the overarching message that God knows all and loves us all passionately. His boundless love gives us courage to risk speaking what is true, certainly to him and hopefully to a few trusted friends. At every conference I see people taking new risks in truth telling. Some situations and faces stay with me for a while.

It was the first conference of 2002. We were in Cincinnati, and the theme was "Sensational Life." At the end of Friday night I stayed at my book table for about an hour talking to people and signing books. As I smiled at the next woman in line I saw a look in her eyes that I recognized. Her eyes told their own story of pain and grief. She seemed to be carrying the weight of the world on her fragile shoulders.

"My son . . . ," she began. "My son was born seven years ago. There was a problem in the delivery, and he was severely brain damaged at birth."

"I'm so sorry," I said, reaching out to hold her arm.

"We seem to have become the poster parents for tragedy overcome by faith. We've been in the newspaper; we've shared our story at church. Everyone tells me what a testimony we are to God's grace. But the truth is, I'm not okay with this unexpected heartache—not at all. When you talked about John the Baptist tonight and said that he wasn't sure that Jesus was the One he had been sent to prepare the way for, I thought that perhaps I wasn't the only one with questions."

I had mentioned the part in Luke's Gospel where John, just before he was beheaded, sent his disciples to Jesus to ask if he was the Messiah or if they should look for another (Luke

7:18–19). It's amazing to consider that the one who had spent his whole life preparing for that one moment when he would say, "Behold the Lamb of God, who takes away the sin of the world," would wonder if he had identified the right Savior. Amazing but encouraging. We are called to follow God even when he doesn't do the things that make sense to us. Jesus sent a message back to John, summing it up with this simple phrase: "God blesses those who are not offended by me" (Luke 7:23 NLT). The message is clear: Will you follow a God you don't understand, who disappoints you, who doesn't answer your prayers the way you would like him to?

"I feel so disloyal," the woman continued. "It's not that I don't love God, but I'm in pain and I wish I could say that without taking away from what people want to hear about our spiritual victory."

"You can!" I assured her. "I think it's far more powerful to tell people what has really happened, how you have struggled and continue to struggle, and yet in the midst of that you love God. That's real and honest. It's true. And it's powerful."

We hugged and as she slipped back into the crowd, I thought again of how harsh we can be to ourselves and to each other. God is not the one who pressures us to be some kind of supersaints. Jesus himself cried out in agony from the cross, "My God, my God, *why* . . . ?"

Being honest is a risky thing. Sometimes others can't handle our honesty; it seems to rock the foundation of their faith. But God welcomes our honesty. It is the hallmark of a trusting heart.

You don't have to pretend with God. Risk being absolutely

honest. Wrestle with your faith. Live your life authentically, always remembering that you are loved forever.

~ *Father, thank you that you welcome me to live a transparent life before you. Thank you that in speaking the truth I can find hope and healing as you shine your light into my dark places. Amen.*

# Big-Hearted Faith

THELMA WELLS

~

*If your first concern is to look after yourself,*
*you'll never find yourself.*
*But if you forget about yourself and look to me,*
*you'll find both yourself and me. (Matthew 10:39 MSG)*

THE LIGHTS WERE TURNED DOWN LOW AS A spotlight shone on the podium atop the massive stage in the Opryland Hotel ballroom. As the speaker of the hour came onstage, his eyes were twinkling, his voice warm and inviting, his body language fluid, his message compelling and challenging. He was Dr. Bruce Wilkinson, the author of the wildly popular book *The Prayer of Jabez.*

Like many people throughout the world, I had read the book and discussed its content and meaning with people whose insights I value. I've given this book as a gift to people after I made sure they had my books first. But there was always a little something I knew was missing for me when I considered this basic, powerful prayer. People say it every day and find that God hears and answers them constantly. I had prayed prayers like this all my life, just not in the words Jabez used in 1 Chronicles 4:10:

Oh, that you would bless me indeed!
Oh, that you would enlarge my territory!
Oh, that your hand would be with me!
Oh, that you would keep me from evil.

The "bless me" part I understood. In fact, I have never had a problem asking the Lord to bless me 'cause he said he would and I believe him. I'm always asking him to keep his hand in mine or to let me rest in his everlasting arms. (I seem to need some part of his body to hold on to.) And "keep me from evil" is a constant prayer 'cause I know me and how out of line I can get sometimes.

But the request in Jabez's prayer that gave me a little trouble was, "Oh, that you would enlarge my territory!" I even read different Scripture versions of this line and found that in some translations of the Bible, in place of the word *territory* were words like *tents, boundaries, coasts,* or *borders.* My dilemma was, *What in the world does this verse really mean?*

After listening to Dr. Wilkinson's message, I no longer have any doubt what it means to me. It means, when you're out on a limb, *go out a little farther.* You see, I discovered from the author that enlarging your territory is really a matter of the heart. "Enlarge the territory, tents, boundaries, coasts, borders of my heart, Lord, so I can work for you the way you intend for me to. Widen my borders, Lord, even though I'm afraid of stepping out of my comfort zone. Raise my tent pegs, Lord, in spite of the fact that I don't know where you are leading me."

I had been dealing with the issue of expansion for nearly two years. God had been encouraging me to spread myself a bit further for him in a ministry that I did *not* have time for 'cause I'm SO BUSY. Yeah, like God didn't know what I was doing every second of my life. Several weeks before I heard Dr. Wilkinson, I had clearly felt God's prompting to enlarge my territory into an arena of mothering and mentoring beyond what I was already doing. I was being led to become a "Mother in Zion" for a particular group of women that includes pastors, evangelists, teachers, apostles, prophetesses, ministry leaders, and pastors' wives. It felt to me like a gigantic leap into risky territory. So I had been hanging out on the limb, making mental excuses for not going any farther. I was trying to figure out, on my own, what I was supposed to do, who I was supposed to include, what location I would use, how I would get the word out without some people feeling excluded . . . all the muckety muck "I" was conjuring up in "my" mind. When I'm on a limb by myself, I usually don't see anybody but me, myself, and I.

Finally, I caved and actually asked *God* what he wanted me to do. Turns out he was just waiting on me to get out of my own way. It became so clear that if I took a little risk, God would give a lot of clarity and direction. He gave me the confidence, commitment, comfort, competence, and contagious excitement to continue moving ahead in what he had called me to do. The Lord enlarged my *heart*—with trust, faith, compassion, hope, drive, tenacity, and LOVE—so I could enter into the adventure before me with joy!

As Dr. Wilkinson ended his message, he invited us to come to the altar and repent of our fears and excuses for not letting the Lord use us in any way he wanted to. "Do your will in me and have your way with me," Dr. Wilkinson suggested we pray.

That invitation is extended to you, too, right where you are. When you take a risk for God, he will be right there beside you, expanding your heart with courage and joy.

～ *God of risks, please take our fears and failures away from us and replace them with trust, faith, and assurance that you will be with us out on the limbs of our lives. Enlarge our hearts, Lord. Amen.*

# The Joy of Boundaries

## MARILYN MEBERG

~

*Make my joy complete by being of the same mind,*
*maintaining the same love, united in spirit,*
*intent on one purpose. (Philippians 2:2 NASB)*

AS A CHILD WATCHING THE CORONATION OF
Queen Elizabeth on our tiny Motorola TV, I fell immediately
in love with the entire royal family. The closest touch of
pageantry my rural community of Amboy, Washington,
offered was when one of Harry Hooper's cows gave birth
inconveniently far from the barn. That occasion would sum-
mon "a few good men" to march into the pasture to return calf
and mother to the barn where they should have been in the
first place. With that accomplished, coffee and hot chocolate
were served in Harry's perennially dirty kitchen.

The image of horse-drawn coronation coaches, diamond-
studded tiaras, Westminster Abbey, and Buckingham Palace
lulled me into a world of glamour dramatically different from
my own. But it was not Queen Elizabeth who captured my
imagination, nor was it the short-lived crush I had on Prince
Philip; it was the queen's little sister, Margaret, who got my
attention. She was purportedly mischievous, rebellious, and

high-spirited. In contrast to the staid and stuffy Elizabeth, I'd choose to have tea with Margaret any day.

As Princess Margaret carried her rebellious nature into adulthood, however, my sense of kinship gave way to disappointment. She became a party girl known for the tortoise-shell cigarette holder she held in one hand and the tumbler of Famous Grouse whiskey in the other. Her life was made up of tortuous romances and unabashed indulgence. "Disobedience is my joy," she told a biographer.

What happened to my childhood "buddy"? What propelled Princess Margaret on a path of such recklessness as she chain-smoked sixty Chesterfields a day, became the first "royal" to divorce in four hundred years, and in a final fling cavorted about with a landscape gardener twenty years younger than she?

Perhaps it was the thrill of taking a dangerous risk—climbing out to the edge of a limb with the rush of knowing it could snap off. Many people give little if any thought to the consequences of this kind of risk-taking. For them, the adrenaline rush is worth the cost. But as believers, we need to ask ourselves a few questions. How far out on the limb will we go? How great a risk will we take? To what degree do we rein ourselves in and refuse the risk? In fact, at what point do we determine that we are no longer contemplating adventure, but disobedience?

The enemy of our souls would love to have us think there is joy in disobedience. Eve fell for that in the Garden. But disobedience does not produce joy, and neither is disobedience adventure. An adventure has an uncertain end; disobedience has a known end. That truth is clearly expressed in Proverbs 14:12: "There is a way which seems right to a man, but its end is the way of death" (NASB).

The good thing about sorting through the risk/adventure issue is that God has made it very clear what our boundaries are to be as we pursue a life of abundance and adventure. In Deuteronomy 10:12–13, appropriate borders for our journey are clearly defined: "What does the LORD your God require of you? He requires you to fear him, to live according to his will, to love and worship him with all your heart and soul, and to obey the LORD's commands and laws" (NLT). God's intent in outlining "requirements" for us was not to eliminate our joy or stifle adventure. He knows our tendency to make poor choices; therefore, to assure our safety and security, he set boundaries for us. When we live within those boundaries, there is joy.

When I read of the death of Princess Margaret I felt nostalgia from my early memories of her and sadness for what she had become. Her life was characterized by a tragic poignancy captured in the headline, "Heartbreak Princess dies of a stroke at age 71." What made me especially sad was that the zest, exuberance, and energy she poured into living were so aimless. She had a great heart for adventure, but she took the wrong risks . . . and, I fear, she missed the joy.

~ *Dear Lord, I thank you that your Word makes it clear when I should tighten the reins and when I can cut loose. Whichever course I take, I choose to love you and worship you with all my heart. Amen.*

# "I Don't Fit"

## SHEILA WALSH

~

*Send forth your light and your truth, let them guide me;*
*let them bring me to your holy mountain,*
*to the place where you dwell. (Psalm 43:3)*

THE PLANE LANDED IN SAN DIEGO WHERE I was to speak at the National Pastors Conference. As I waited at the carousel for my bags, I found myself thinking back to a conversation that took place more than twenty-five years ago. In my mind I was back in Ayr, Scotland, sitting in the kitchen of our pastor's home. His wife was a dear friend, full of life and fun; but I had noticed recently that she seemed troubled.

"Is everything all right?" I asked.

"Oh, I'm fine," she replied with a sigh, passing me another cup of tea.

"You don't sound fine."

"Well, sometimes I feel as if I don't fit, as if I am a disappointment here," she confided.

"What do you mean? You are awesome!" I replied with the passion of an intense teenager.

"I'm not the traditional pastor's wife," she said.

"That must be why we all love you!"

"Thanks, but I don't think everyone shares your heart on

this. There are certain things I'm supposed to do or want to be. I try, but it's just not me."

I remember the look in her eyes. I saw the pain of wanting to meet the expectations of others, the desire to stand side by side with her husband in ministry, and yet the pressure of the unspoken but weighty disapproval of some who wanted a more traditional pastor's wife who would lead the women's meetings and serve on every church committee.

My bags arrived and I headed off to the hotel. I had three sessions the next day. I was part of a lunchtime panel discussion; I had a two-hour seminar in the afternoon; and I was the speaker at the evening session. The session that impacted me most was the afternoon seminar. My advertised subject in the brochure was "Living Honestly Before God." The seminars were optional, so I had no idea how many would show up. When I arrived at the classroom I saw that it was filled to the brim with a few pastors and a lot of pastors' wives.

For the first hour and a half I shared my own story of my struggle to be honest and real in the midst of public ministry; then I opened up the remaining time for questions and discussion. After a few questions about my own journey, a woman stood up at the back of the room and said with tears running down her cheeks, "I'm tired of trying to be what everyone else in the church thinks I should be. I don't fit. My trouble is that I don't even want to fit."

One by one, women stood and shared similar feelings. I sat down and listened as they reached out to one another with the deep empathy of those who walk a similar path. Some of the older women told how they had struggled in the early years of their husbands' calling and what they had learned along the way.

"I thought I was the only one who felt like this," someone said. Laughter rippled over the crowd.

"Me, too!"

"This is great!"

"Can you all move to our church?"

When the session was over several of us stayed for a while and talked about the peculiar pressures of those in the ministry spotlight.

That evening as I lay in a hot bath I thought again about my friend in Scotland. She has found a new freedom and joy ministering to women who live on the streets of Glasgow, selling their bodies to pay for a drug habit or to support children on their own. She has found where she fits, and she loves it.

As I thought about her and prayed for some of the women I had listened to that day, I realized that this is a problem that is not particular to pastors' wives. We all long to fit in. We long for approval. Sometimes that very hunger can drive us to walk around in ill-fitting shoes. It takes courage to map out our own trail and find ways of living our lives and serving God that are a perfect fit for us.

I went to seminary to train to be a missionary to India, but it didn't take long to realize that was not what I wanted to do. It was actually what I thought I would hate, but I erroneously assumed that "sacrificing" myself by doing what I perceived as the ultimate Christian ministry would win the approval of God and others. I risked letting go of that self-imposed ideal and soon found myself on a new path as the first female evangelist with Youth for Christ. And that was just the beginning of all God had in mind for me.

Are there things you long to do but are afraid of? Then pray with the psalmist David, "Send forth your light and your truth; let them guide me." It can feel risky to set aside old ideas and expectations, but when we move forward with the aid of divine guidance, we will discover our true calling.

~ *Father God, today I ask that you would light my path and guide my steps. Grant me the courage to live the life that you have uniquely prepared me for. Amen.*

# To Scowl or Not to Scowl

## MARILYN MEBERG

~

*Charm is deceitful and beauty is vain, but a woman who fears the*
*LORD, she shall be praised. (Proverbs 31:30 NASB)*

THERE IS APPARENTLY A GROWING NUMBER OF
the facially discontent in our world. These are the people who
peer myopically into the mirror and experience a degree of
dismay or even horror at the image staring back. "When did
this happen and who gave it permission?" we ask the image.
The image, if an especially cheeky one, may quip, "You're getting old, baby . . . and it's becoming increasingly obvious;
people are noticing."

My father was a great fan of the comedian Jack Benny, who
said age is strictly a case of mind over matter. If you don't
mind, it doesn't matter. I don't agree with that at all! Of course
I mind. But to what degree do I mind? Would I consider anything as major as a face-lift to quiet the cheeky mirror image?
I'd love to look younger, but all too often the result of a face-
lift looks as if a mighty wind has swept the flesh back behind
the ears, leaving a facial expression of frozen perplexity. I also
don't like pain, especially if I have chosen it.

Modern experts on the fountain of youth assure me there
is no need for fear of pain or of a "bad result" to hold me back,

however. The very simple solution is to take poison. It's cheaper, less painful, and has been FDA-approved. I'm talking botox—the most potent of all known biological toxins.

In spite of its ominous potential to paralyze or kill, botox has become the most popular method for wrinkle control. The drug is injected directly into the "offensive" area, where it blocks the signals between nerves and muscle, paralyzing the muscle and stopping its pulling and crinkling on the overlying skin. The new "in" social activity in California is a botox party. You gather up some good friends, drop into your local plastic surgeon's office, get your injections, and then chat about your experiences over lavish offerings of food and drink set up for your gala. Good grief!

You may be comforted to know that the impact of botox is not bodywide but limited to the muscle into which it has been injected. For that reason one cannot become paralyzed or suffer respiratory failure from proper treatment. Another bit of happy news, experts say, is that botox is metabolized within hours, so it doesn't accumulate in the body.

Now, here's the downside of poisoning yourself: Treatments run from $200 to $500, and the effects wear off after four to six months. There's a personal downside for me apart from the money and the need to get repeat injections. The chief targets of botox are the vertical furrows between the brows and horizontal lines on the forehead. According to botox enthusiasts, I can expect the virtual disappearance of frown lines. In fact, after botox therapy on a brow muscle I won't be able to knit my brow when I talk to my tax man or scowl at the woman beside me who whispers to her neighbor throughout the movie. With botox I will become frown impaired. I will look as if I'm having a perpetually good day whether I am or not!

The issue of cosmetic alteration is not a spiritual problem as I see it. If we do or do not choose to scowl does not affect God's acceptance of us. But here's my point: Would it not be an incredible relief to no longer be preoccupied or worried about how we appear? To not care about the wrinkles, the tummy pooch, or the flapping of ever-loosening flesh? Wouldn't it be an adventure into a world both foreign and delightful to toss our cosmetic bags aside and concern ourselves with hygiene only? (There is a limit to being "natural"; can't get rid of the soap or toothbrush.) What if we had the freedom to jump out of bed in the morning, run a comb through our hair, and take off for the day? Are you game for such an adventure?

Of course you're not; neither am I. But you have to admit, it's a compelling idea. Wouldn't it be a great adventure to sincerely toss aside all our image concerns and face the world exactly as we are, convinced that wrinkles are not blemishes?

Ava Gardner once said of her wrinkles, "My face looks . . . well . . . lived in." So does mine . . . and I think I'll keep it that way—scowlability intact.

~ *Lord, your Word reminds me that you see the heart of each person. Appearance means nothing to you. May I see as you see—especially the image in my own mirror. Amen.*

# Take a Risk . . . and Share the Gift

## BARBARA JOHNSON

~

*He gives strength to the weary and*
*increases the power of the weak. (Isaiah 40:29)*

I'VE GIVEN UP ON THE IDEA OF BEING A MIS-
sionary in darkest Africa. It's also unlikely I'll ever make it to
India to do God's work in the orphanages there. I probably
won't make it to China, either, risking punishment by handing out Bibles in some secret place. But I can be a missionary,
nonetheless. And I'll still be taking risks.

Right from my home, I can be a missionary to the discouraged, those who are tired and weary, uncertain about the
future, and wondering if anybody cares about them. And I can
share the gift of laughter with those who've lost their joy.
Sounds easy and "safe" enough, doesn't it? But let me assure
you, after being involved in an outreach ministry for many
years, there are risks involved! Even when we reach out to others with comforting words or thoughtful deeds, our actions
can be misunderstood, our intentions can be misinterpreted,
and the result can be harsh and hurtful responses.

There have been days when I've opened fifty love-filled, laugh-
ter-lined letters—but find myself obsessed with that one small
note of complaint or condemnation, perhaps about a joke I told

that someone considered inappropriate or about my efforts to encourage parents to love and accept their homosexual children.

For example, I used to tell about our son Tim having a job at the nearby mortuary when he was a teenager. He was always bringing home some little memento of his work, so I got used to seeing our dog wearing a ribbon around its neck that said, "God Bless Grandpa Hyrum." I shared that memory when I was speaking to a women's group somewhere and soon afterward got a letter from a woman who said she was shocked that I'd think it was funny that Tim was bringing home *bones* from the mortuary.

I quickly gave the woman a call. "It wasn't *bones,*" I told her emphatically. "It was bows—*bows* off some of the floral arrangements."

I'm still not sure she understood. That's one of the risks we take whenever we try to communicate. We can be misunderstood, and as a result, we can be hurt. It's distressing to send out a message of love and have it angrily thrown back in our faces. But it's the risk we take whenever we interact with other human beings, and it's important to keep trying as we trust God to guide our message to those who need to hear it most.

Several times when I've contacted someone who's written me a harsh letter, criticizing me for something I've said or done, the experience has turned out to be totally rewarding. For example, I once included a story in one of my books that inadvertently hurt someone who thought the story reflected badly on her. I had permission to use the story, and it really wasn't about her at all. But it was about someone she loved, and she contacted my publisher, expressing concern that her loved one's reputation—and her own—could be damaged.

I dreaded doing it, but I called her, and we talked for nearly an hour. At the end of the conversation, she thanked me for taking the time to call. I thanked her for reading my book! We've been friends ever since, and she has become a contributor to our ministry.

Take a risk. Reach out to someone. Let Isaiah 40:29 remind you that God enables us to do his work—so surely he enables us also to deal with the results, whatever they are. You may be rebuffed. You may even get hurt in the process. But it's worth the risk. Because by reaching out, sharing God's love, and spreading the good news of his Word, you might make a new friend. You might even change someone's life for eternity.

~ *Dear Jesus, thank you for the risk you took, the pain you endured, to reach out to me and lead me into paradise. Help me to be brave in loving as you loved. Amen.*

# Let There Be Paint!

## SHEILA WALSH

~

*In the beginning God created the heavens and the earth. Now the earth was formless and empty, darkness was over the surface of the deep, and the Spirit of God was hovering over the waters. And God said, "Let there be light," and there was light. (Genesis 1:1–3)*

OUR WOMEN OF FAITH CONFERENCE SCHEDULE usually runs from February/March until November, giving us December and January to relax, recharge our batteries, and, for me, an excuse to eat anything I want knowing that I don't have to fit into a suit for weeks. I recharge by staying in my jammies for about two weeks with a pint of Häagen Dazs ice cream in each hand, hair sticking up like cacti caught in a tsunami. I don't go out. My friends know that they are welcome to come over, but they have to take me as I am. One dear friend comes each year with a camera, threatening to sell the photos to *Christianity Today*. "Go ahead!" I say. "If God can speak through an ass he can surely speak through a pj-clad, no-makeup, train-wreck of a Scotswoman!" So far she hasn't had any offers for the photos!

My husband, Barry, does not do well with downtime. He gets antsy to do something creative. Christian and I try to respectfully avoid him in case we get roped in. In the winter of 2002, Barry became Paint Man. He decided overnight that every wall in our house needed to be painted a different color. He set off for the hardware store like a soldier who had heard the call to be all he can be. He returned with ladders, paint, drop cloths, brushes, and a burning passion in his eyes. Christian offered to help. Barry had seen some of Christian's painting projects and politely declined.

"But I want to paint, too, Mom," he said. "I can help. I'm a helper."

What to do? I stumbled upon a perfect compromise, or so I thought.

"Why don't we paint your room?" I suggested. Then I followed up with this ridiculous question: "What color do you want to paint it?" (Never ask a five-year-old boy what color he wants to paint his room!) He wanted it blue with yellow polka dots and green stripes.

"All of it?" I asked, hoping that he would say, "No, just the closet."

"All of it," he replied with hearty conviction. "Every wall."

And so we began. We put drop cloths over the cream carpet and the cat, put on our oldest jeans and T-shirts, and went wild.

I mentioned this project in my newsletter that I send out every week and was amazed by the response. Some wrote to say that they wished they had allowed their kids to do this when they were young. Some shared stories of their own home "improvement" projects and the memories they had made as a family. One woman wrote a brief note: "Go for it; it's only paint!" I loved that.

The more I thought about it, the more I celebrated the fact that this is how God is with each of us. The great Master Painter allows you and me to take up our little brushes and paint our lives in a multitude of colors—some that clash, some that take others by surprise or provoke disapproval. In all of this he looks down on us in love, he smiles, he celebrates our uniqueness.

When Christian took up his brush, I was there, as was his daddy. We put plastic down to catch the drips. We advised a little here and there, but we enjoyed the whole experience and took lots of photos. Too often we play it safe in life because we're afraid of making mistakes. But God is a God of color, of light. He is creative and spectacular in every way. He doesn't hold back in his self-expression!

So take risks with your kids. Do crazy things. Surprise your husband. Have dinner all set up in the yard with candles and music. Dress in a whole new style. Change your hairstyle or color. Paint a wall—every wall! If you've seen the television show *The Magic School Bus,* you'll remember Miss Frizzel's motto: "Take chances, get messy, make mistakes." Amen, Miss Frizzel!

~ *Father God, Creator of light and shadow, of night and day, of sunsets and storms, give me a fresh vision of the beauty of your world as well as a deep appreciation for your creative imprint on my own soul. Thank you for your invitation to participate fully and boldly in my life, knowing that you walk right beside me in all the moments and messes. Amen.*

# Part 5

~

## TAKING THE PLUNGE:

### DIVE INTO LIFE . . . C'MON, DO IT!

# Playful Pleasures

### LUCI SWINDOLL

~

*My chosen ones will long enjoy the
works of their hands. (Isaiah 65:22)*

PLAYFULNESS. I LOVE THAT QUALITY. PLAYFUL
people look at life through a kaleidoscopic lens, seeing all
kinds of ways to find adventure and have fun. They've
unlocked the door to the child within, and they're always
looking for something with which to play—a sight, a sound,
a person, an idea. The interesting thing is that they're from all
walks of life—the executive, the waitress, the bus driver, the
attorney, the gas station attendant, the doctor, the minister,
the hairdresser, the street person, and the guy who lives in that
high-rise over there.

This child within each of us is the muse for our creativity,
the catalyst for our joy, and the spirit behind our wildest
dreams. Our inner child wants to dawdle, putter, explore,
enjoy, and make up things. It doesn't matter if they are pretty
things or formed correctly. What matters is the pleasure that
comes as the result of our creative efforts.

With the onslaught of life's demands and duties, some of us
forget to be playful. We keep our inner child hidden, "proper"
and in line, and we forget that it is she who can provide the

enjoyment we long for in daily life. Pablo Picasso put it wisely: "Every child is an artist. The problem is how to remain an artist once that child grows up." Ah yes! There's the rub.

My adult person has built a little room in my house where my inner child comes out to play: *The Studio*. It is a forty-two-square-foot dream machine. It's painted yellow and crammed full of books, toys, paints, clay, stickers, stamps, and games. It has a small drafting table with chair, a baby radio, and boxes of treasures. Originally, it was the walk-in clothes closet for my bedroom, but how badly do I need a clothes closet? More important, I need a place to play jacks. And I do!

Last night I went in there and blew bubbles. Somebody gave me a little jar of "Miracle Bubbles" with a plastic wand . . . and I blew bubbles for maybe ten minutes. (A few weeks ago I made a new wand with the shape of a cat on the end. I wanted to see if the bubbles would come out cat-shaped. They don't). That tiny room where I play and paint and putter brings me tremendous pleasure. I'm even branching out now . . . I've taken over the linen closet and pantry for more fun places for Little Luci to have her say. Soon, I'm going into the yard.

Maybe you'd like to have your inner child come outside and enjoy a bit of adventure, but you don't quite know how to coax her forth. After all, you're grown up, have a respectable job where you wear business clothes every day, have worked hard for your education, and don't want to look like an idiot by acting like a child blowing bubbles. You don't have time to be creative or playful. It takes all the energy you can muster just to get through your busy day at the office. If you let down your decorum, what will people think?

I can tell you what they'll think. They'll be jealous that you've found a way to take the drudge out of the daily grind. They'll want to know why you can't wipe that smile off your face. They'll want what you have. They'll ask where you unearthed the fountain of youth and what you're drinking from it. *Everybody wants to be where the fun is.* I don't know a single person who is having too much fun.

Here are a half dozen tips that may help bring your muse into the sunlight:

- Figure out what the child within you wants to do and do it.

- Listen to that tiny, soft voice inside and believe it.

- Quit conforming to what the world demands and say, "No!" (Kids are good at that.)

- Surround yourself with people who love you and enjoy them.

- Create a life for yourself that's meaningful and live there.

- Keep in mind that imagination is more important than knowledge.

These six things won't get you to heaven or make you debt free or fill in all the gaps in your needy soul, but they will give you a start in gaining victory over some of the enemies with which you wage war all too often—boredom, anxiety, cynicism, stress, and procrastination. These little tips have worked for seven decades, and even now I'm still learning about the little person inside me who wants to come out and play.

More than two thousand years ago, Jesus said to a crowd of people gathered around him, "Unless you change and become like little children, you will never enter the kingdom of heaven" (Matthew 18:3). The truth of that is something we all need to remember today in our busy, rat-race lives.

Don't be afraid to explore playful pleasures in your life. Let them spill outside the bounds of your leisure and work, your home and office, your school and church. Let them permeate your life. And the next time somebody asks for a volunteer to be a clown at the block party, raise your hand.

~ *I praise you, Father, that I am your child. Thank you for giving me the freedom to play and experiment and risk and have fun. Show me a way to take pleasure in my life today. Amen.*

# The Water's Great

PATSY CLAIRMONT

~

*And God saw that it was good. (Genesis 1:10)*

WHEN WAS THE LAST TIME YOU TRIED SOMETHING outside your comfort zone? I'm not thinking of anything as radical as bulging your corneas with bungee jumping. No, I have in mind expanding your sense of yourself in an artistic adventure.

Not an artist you say? Yup, I see all those hands. I know how you feel. My stick figures are in physical therapy even as we speak. But much to my amazement, I've tried some art forms in which my creative expression has surprised and pleased me.

First thing to do before plunging into a new pool of endeavor is to test the water. We do that by asking ourselves what we haven't explored that interests us.

I have a number of friends who have tried their hands at painting. Some chose watercolors, others oils, while still others dabbled with acrylics. Across the board they had wonderful results. All of them had very different styles, yet their art was fine enough to be featured in their homes. In fact, I'm delighted to say several of their pictures hang in my home.

My friend Will found himself unexpectedly retired and needed a pastime. He took up whittling. He started with caricature cowboys and graduated to exquisite, carved clocks.

Likewise, my husband, Les, was forced into retirement because of his health when he was forty-seven years old—not what he had planned. One day he announced he was going to take a stained-glass class. Well, you could have knocked me over with a feather; he had never mentioned any artistic interest before. But I was even more surprised by the stunning results. Since then I've been the grateful recipient of many beautiful lamps and stained-glass garden stones created by my gifted husband.

My niece Kelly enjoyed creative stamping; she made darling cards and beautiful scrapbooks. She loved it so much that she helped other women learn charming ways to personalize their gifts, books, and notes with stamping. That grew into Kelly's designing her own stamps and starting a business. Way to dive into the pool, Kelly!

My friend Debbie has a teenage daughter who was given a school assignment that required her to render a drawing. The teachers were so taken with her obvious giftedness that they contacted her mom. Debbie was taken, too—taken aback. She had no idea of her daughter's gift.

C'mon, let's consider splashing around in a new pool to discover sides of ourselves we haven't yet discovered. Perhaps painting, whittling, or stamping isn't your thing, but maybe you like to decorate. I do. I love to give a fresh look to tired surroundings. The room becomes a canvas and the furniture my paints. Friends sometimes let me play artist in a room they are sick of in hopes that I can show them a new perspective.

Do you enjoy photography? I visited Luci, a real shutterbug, for advice on what kind of camera to invest in. And I have loved the results. I now flutter about clicking flowers in my garden and the cutest little sweet pea of all, my grandson, Justin. Sometimes I only get one picture out of a whole roll that's worth framing, but that's why photographers take so many shots from so many angles. Don't give up; you may be one roll away from a prize winner!

Still nothing rings your creative chimes? Are you a good cook? Now, honey, that's artistry everyone will applaud. My friend Carol is a culinary genius. When she calls to invite us for dinner, we're in her driveway before she hangs up the phone.

Do you set an attractive table? Are you good with a glue gun, a power drill, or a jigsaw? Do you have an organizational touch? Are you able to paint pictures with words? Can you strum a mandolin, sing like a lark, style hair, arrange flowers, crochet tablecloths, design jewelry, or quilt? If you said no to all the above, then I would ask you, are you sure? If you haven't tried, how do you know?

We owe it to ourselves to make room for artistic expression. After all, the creative process puts us in touch with the Creator. I think Christ's growing up around a carpenter dad affirms the significance of working with our hands, especially when it's an outgrowth of what's in our hearts.

Here's your adventure assignment: Find a creative endeavor and dive in!

~ *Father, did it thrill you to see the waters form into oceans and lakes? Were you delighted with the chiseled mountains and the watercolor sunsets? Did you whittle out the canyons? And carpet the valley floor in lavender and Queen Anne's lace? Your artistry is breathtaking and inspiring. Thank you for making us in your image. Help us to enter into our days with enthusiasm and flair. Amen.*

# "The Dog Won't Fly!"

## SHEILA WALSH

~

*You have filled my heart with greater joy*
*than when their grain and new wine abound.*
*I will lie down and sleep in peace, for you alone,*
*O LORD, make me dwell in safety. (Psalm 4:7–8)*

IT WAS A NEW EXPERIENCE FOR ME. I HAD no idea if I would be able to do it. I volunteered out of ignorance, and when the day arrived I was stunned by my naiveté.

"What was I thinking?" I said out loud in the cab as I traveled to the church.

"Can I help you, ma'am?" the driver asked.

"Can you dance?" I replied.

"Not much," he said.

"Well, me neither . . . so now what?"

He returned to concentrating on driving, glad to be about to unload the nut case in the backseat.

It started so innocently. I wanted to write books for children. I actually started writing for my own son, and the vision grew into a series of five books published by Waterbrook Press under the banner "Children of Faith." Integrity Music expressed interest in partnering with us, and soon we had a CD. Tommy Nelson caught the vision and we had an animated movie. I was very excited. Then there was talk of a Christmas tour.

"This will be so fun," I said to Barry. "We can all go. Christian has never toured on a bus before. It'll be great. We'll get a tree and lights for the bus and make it a winter wonderland!"

In no time I was sitting at a conference table with all interested parties.

"Will you be in the tour?" the prospective tour producer asked.

"Sure, if you want me to be," I said too quickly.

"That would be great," he said. And suddenly it was a done deal.

I didn't think much more about it. I was busy with Women of Faith conferences, and Thanksgiving seemed a long way away. But as it edged closer I got the first in a series of unexpected calls.

"We'll need you in Dallas for one week of dance rehearsals. And one week in Nashville, too," the director said.

"Dance rehearsals? Dance rehearsals? What are you talking about? I can't dance. I was raised a Baptist!" I told him, beads of sweat breaking out on my forehead.

"You have the main part in this show," he informed me politely. "The other characters are in large animal costumes. You are our human."

"I don't want to be a human. Can't I be the ostrich or the monkey?" I begged.

"No."

The cab pulled up outside Prestonwood Baptist Church.

The irony did not go unnoticed. I was introduced to the other actors and dancers, all in their twenties. I watched them warm up and stretch in ways I haven't since I gave birth.

"For your first move, bend down, jump as high as you can, and you will end up on my shoulder," Matt said.

"On your shoulder!" I uttered incredulously. "I'm not a parrot."

At the end of the first day and ten hours of jumping around like a manic squirrel, I was exhausted.

"We're off to the gym, do you want to come?" Julie asked.

"Gym! I want the emergency room!"

Somehow I survived the first week, and as the second week approached its end, opening night reared its ugly head like a date for a root canal. Everything that could go wrong went wrong. Wrong set pieces were delivered, costumes didn't fit; but it all came to a head on the day after Thanksgiving. Opening night was the following evening, and I was still short two pieces of my costume. Have you ever tried to hurry through a mall on the biggest shopping day of the year looking for a purple wig and a feather boa? Suddenly, in the middle of a lynch mob of determined buyers, my cell phone rang.

"The dog won't fly!" the voice cried out.

"What do you mean?" I asked.

"It won't fly. The dog says it's not safe. The dog won't fly!"

I started to laugh. I laughed so hard I had tears running down my face, and I had to hold on to a confused shopper in front of me. She started to laugh; her husband joined in. Soon I was standing in a circle of people who were all laughing and didn't have a clue why.

"Why are we laughing?" the woman asked.

"The . . . the . . . the dog won't fly," I spat out like a sparkler on the Fourth of July. It made no sense to them, but it did wonders for me.

I returned to the set with the wig and the boa. We made sure that the dog had enough rehearsal time to be comfortable flying. I adjusted the dancing and jumps to fit my forty-five-year-old body, and we had a wonderful time. It was outside my comfort zone. Way outside. But I survived and had so much fun.

How long has it been since you've done something that stretches you? You don't have to be great at it; it's just fun to participate vigorously in life. The dancers in my show got many laughs watching me attempt to land on Matt's shoulder. I never did make it, but I had fun trying.

It's easy to lose joy in life. We get to the stage where we take ourselves too seriously or are afraid to make mistakes. But when we know that we are loved by God, loved beyond measure, we can dive in and take a chance. Success or failure doesn't matter. We showed up, and that's all it takes.

~ *Father, thank you for the security that your love brings to my life. Teach me to dive into life with passion and joy, knowing that you will be there to catch me if I fall. In Jesus' name, amen.*

# A Fish Out of Water

THELMA WELLS

~

*It will come about that every living creature which
swarms in every place where the river goes, will live.
And there will be very many fish, for these waters
go there and the others become fresh; so everything
will live where the river goes. (Ezekiel 47:9 NASB)*

MY FRIEND GWEN RETIRED AS AN EDUCATOR
in the 1990s. She had been a teacher, counselor, and assistant
principal for more than thirty-five years. Competent, confident, personable, articulate, fashionable, and Miss Personality
Plus, Gwen often told me how she enjoyed her profession but
felt there was something missing in her life. It was not Christ
because she had been a Christian since we were little girls
growing up together and attending the same church.

After Gwen retired, she began an earnest quest to discover
her destiny. She dabbled in real estate, sales, accounting, care-
taking, volunteering, writing, proofreading, cake baking, tutoring,
marketing. She was willing to try almost anything . . . but she
still felt like a live fish out of water, floundering, flittering, and
trying to fin its way back to the freedom of its natural habitat.

Eventually, she established an accounting business with
office, computer, shingle and all. She sat for several weeks call-

ing, praying, looking, and begging for clients. Nobody came. The rent was due, the phone was on, the computer programs were installed; but she had no business. How disappointing to invest your time, energy, money, talents, and husband's patience in something that isn't working.

A few months later, Gwen surprised a group of us when she reported that she was finally completely at peace about her purpose in life. After much reflection, she told us, she'd realized that many of her ventures had seemed for naught because she did not seize the moment to speak up for God wherever she was. When she did take opportunities to share God's truth and love, she felt total satisfaction. Gwen finally understood, without a doubt, that all her life God had been "calling" her to be a verbal witness for him—whether she was teaching, counseling, selling, being an entrepreneur or homemaker or *whatever*.

I admire Gwen's tenacity. I rejoice with her that after more than six decades she finally discovered what she wants to be when she grows up. The fish finally found her pool of satisfaction.

I feel fortunate that it didn't take me that long to find my river of purpose. I, too, was an educator with a degree in secondary education. After teaching for nearly two years in a high school in Dallas, I realized that teaching children was not my life's calling. I then worked in the farm-implement industry for nearly five years and discovered that wasn't my life's calling either. I stayed at home and become a "domestic engineer," playing the role of mama, wife, maid, baker, cook, gardener, day-care provider, lover . . . you know, all the stuff that I admire about many women but can't tolerate for myself as a full-time vocation. Obviously, that alone was not my life's calling.

Then I thought I had finally found it. I became a banker and a trainer for the advancement of other bankers. For twelve years I poured all my professional efforts into being the best banker who ever counted a dollar bill or managed a group of money handlers. But there was still something missing in my life, as there was in Gwen's. During those years I prayed for God to lead me to the pool of freedom and satisfaction that he had filled for me before I was even born.

At the age of thirty-nine I finally found out what I was created to do. I had been encouraging, inspiring, influencing, and empowering people to BEE their best for about four years. The fulfillment and completeness I felt when I was speaking to groups was totally satisfying. However, it presented a challenge for me because I was working full-time as a banker and trainer; I was busy being the wife, mother, church woman, civic leader, and whatever else I thought I needed to do to create the kind of life I wanted for myself and my family. But there came a time when I knew I had to take the plunge into deeper waters if I was to be truly satisfied and please God.

The urge to leave my secure and prestigious position as assistant vice president of the largest independent bank in Texas was overwhelming. Considering *actually* leaving presented a great dilemma, however. So, I took a yellow legal pad and several pencils and marched myself to a cafeteria in the mall next to the bank. I sat in the farthest corner I could find where there was some peace and quiet and I drew a "T" formation on a sheet of paper. I wrote "Advantages" to staying in my current job on one side and "Disadvantages" on the other.

On another sheet of paper I wrote "Advantages" and "Disadvantages" of leaving my job. Under each column I wrote everything I could think of that fit into those four categories.

After I had exhausted my options on those topics, I posed another scenario on paper: "Worst case if I stay in my job" and "Worst case if I leave my job." It took time to really think through and write down all the worst-case scenarios I could think of. Some of them didn't even make sense, but I wrote down everything I thought or feared.

Then I moved to what I believe was the most critical question of all: "In five years, will it make a difference to me if I stay in my job or if I leave?" The immediate answer was very informative. YES! If I stayed in my job I would never know if I could make it in the inspirational-speaking business. YES! In my heart of hearts, I *knew* God wanted me to speak for him. YES! Even if I failed (as some call failure) I would know, without a doubt, that I had done what I was born to do.

On August 17, 1984, I left my position at the bank to become a full-time inspirational speaker. In spite of the occasional heartaches and disappointments of this career, the results of doing what God has assigned me have never caused me to flitter, flap, and flounder in search of different waters. I finally found the river of contentment that comes from being in the stream of God's perfect will.

~ *Master of our destiny, please help us to understand what pool you want us to swim in, the wisdom to search for it, and the courage to take the plunge. Help us to "just do it!" Amen.*

# Dance the Night Away

SHEILA WALSH

~

*You turned my wailing into dancing;*
*you removed my sackcloth and clothed me with joy,*
*that my heart may sing to you and not be silent.*
*O LORD my God, I will give you thanks forever.*
*(Psalm 30:11–12)*

BE IN THE CHURCH PARKING LOT AT 6:15 P.M.
sharp. Wear casual clothes, bring finger foods, and don't forget your dancing shoes. Christian can come, too."

I listened to the message on my answering machine a
couple of times to make sure I wasn't hearing things. I asked
Barry to listen to it, too.

"What do you think it means?" I asked.

"Well, Sue's in charge tonight, so it could mean anything,"
he replied.

"Good point," I said, smiling at the thought of the wacky
antics of our friend.

The small group that Barry, Christian, and I belong to in
our church is somewhat unconventional. I think that's why we
were invited to join. We meet at one of our homes every
Sunday night. We bring food. We laugh and tell jokes and
catch up with what kind of week everyone has had. We pray for

each other in the midst of crushing loss and heartache. We celebrate the joy of a new baby, the launch of a new book, God's hand of blessing and favor on our children, or that final stubborn ten pounds exercised into oblivion. We share all of life.

This particular Sunday evening was an adventure. We were the first to arrive, then Jean and Bill. It was the first time we had seen Jean since she had been released from the hospital after a terrible accident. She looked wonderful.

"Do you know where we're going?" I asked.

"No clue!" she said. "Knowing Sue, it should be quite a trip."

Finally, we were all present and accounted for. "Keep an eye on the car in front and the car behind," Sue said as a convoy of fifteen cars moved out of the parking lot like a lethargic nocturnal python. We drove out into the dark winter countryside.

"Is that the same car we were following?" I asked Barry as we tried to catch up after being stranded at a red light.

"I think so," he said.

"I hope so or this guy will wonder why we are following him home."

"Where are we going, Mom?" a little voice inquired from the backseat.

"I don't know," I said.

"Then why are we going?"

"It's an adventure!" I replied.

At last we pulled into a residential neighborhood and stopped outside a house. Music was pulsing through the walls and lights were flickering on and off. I stood on the front lawn and peered in the window.

"Barry. Look at this. It's a disco ball!" I said as I watched a single beam of light hit the suspended silver globe and become a million tiny dancing stars. Barry and I are one of the younger couples in our group. Several are in their fifties and sixties so the thought of a Sunday night version of *Saturday Night Fever* would never have occurred to me.

Sue explained. "My brother and his wife had a party last night for their daughter's sixteenth birthday. I asked him to leave all the stuff up so we could have some fun of our own tonight."

For a moment we all stood like a herd of deer caught in the headlights of a Mac truck. We are from varied denominational backgrounds that presented inevitable questions as to whether or not this was a sacred option on the Lord's Day. My old Baptist question, "What if the Lord returns during 'Boogie Oogie Oogie'?" presented itself, soon to be dismissed by the glorious, ridiculous joy of laughing, dancing, and looking completely silly together. Others in our group were simply wondering if their bifocals could cope with the strobe lights.

I'll never forget that night. I can still see my five-year-old son dancing round and round with two of our friends in their sixties, one the survivor of breast cancer, the other of the loss of a husband and a son. Those who couldn't dance or had no desire to stood round the edges laughing and enjoying the efforts of those who threw themselves in whether they could dance or not. I thought later of all the moments when we had wept together, walked through dark moments or months, and held one another when grief was fresh and powerful. Those moments and memories made the laughter and silliness all the sweeter.

How long has it been since you surprised your family and friends with something outside the box of what is the norm for you and them? What I experienced that Sunday night was that trust makes risk possible. When we have walked through tough times together, stood by one another, we can take risks together, too. We can dive into the deep end of both sorrow and joy and know that we will come out all right.

Dare to be the one who's willing to throw the party so that others can dust off their dancing shoes and laugh again.

*~ Father, thank you for life, for friends, for tears and laughter. Remind me today that life is precious and short. I don't want to spend my days living in fear or doubt. Help me to dive into my life, no matter what it holds. Amen.*

# Go Ahead, Jump!

## BARBARA JOHNSON

~

*You answer us in amazing ways,*
*God our Savior. People everywhere on*
*the earth and beyond the sea trust you. (Psalm 65:5 NCV)*

A WOMAN ACCOMPANIED HER HUSBAND TO
the doctor's office for a checkup. Afterward, the physician
asked to speak to the wife alone. He told her, "Your husband
has a serious problem. Unless you do the following things for
him, he will surely die. First, you need to make sure he gets a
good, healthy breakfast every morning. Then, have him come
home for lunch every day and feed him a well-balanced meal.
Make sure you feed him a good, hot, nutritious dinner every
night. Also, you must keep the house spotless and clean so he
won't be exposed to any unnecessary germs. And finally, don't
burden him with household chores."

As they settled into the car for the ride home, the husband
asked his wife, "Well, what did the doctor tell you about my
condition?"

The wife replied, "He said you're going to die."

As a wife who gave up cooking long ago and who consid-
ers dust a decorative item, I laugh every time I hear that story.
Oddly enough, Bill doesn't think it's funny. Perhaps that's

because he recently survived a year when the roles in our marriage were completely reversed. During my yearlong bout with a malignant brain tumor, Bill did all the housework, managed to keep us both fed nutritiously (as long as you consider hot dogs and popcorn nutritious), and also made sure I followed the chemotherapy regimen to the letter. There were times when he would show up beside my chair or my bed with a plate of food or a pile of pills, and I simply trusted him to know what I needed to do.

The experience reminded me of when my granddaughters were young, about five and seven, and Barney, my son, would bring them to our house to swim in our pool. They loved to sit on the edge, dangling their feet in the water, and watch their dad perform a special show for them—crazy jumps, elegant dives, big-splash cannonballs.

Ah, but then it was *their* turn. Barney would stand them up on the edge of the pool and coax them to jump into the water. They nervously twisted and squirmed, wringing their little hands and scrunching their sweet faces into contortions of anxiety. Barney would stand in the water just a few feet in front of them, saying, "Trust me. I'll catch you, and I won't let your head go under water. Just trust me to catch you."

But before they jumped, they wanted to make sure Barney was able and prepared for his duty. "Are you ready, Daddy? Are you sure you can catch me?" they would ask. "What if you miss? What if you drop me?"

"I won't miss. I'm standing right here. I won't drop you. Trust me," Barney would say again.

"Okay, Daddy, here I come. Are you really ready?"

"I'm ready."

"Really, really, *really* ready?"

"You can do it, honey. Jump!"

And finally, one by one, they did. They leaped into their father's big, strong arms, and he caught them and hugged them with congratulatory glee. "You did it!" Then he would swirl them through the water the way they loved, a little bonus for being so brave.

After that, they would climb out of the water, poise once more on the edge, and begin the whole procedure over again. Eventually, the whining pleas became part of the fun, a dramatic act performed with glee before an audience of one—Grandma Barb.

Watching their performance, I couldn't help but realize I was seeing an earthly demonstration of our heavenly Father's promise. "Trust in the LORD with all your heart," Scripture tells us (Proverbs 3:5). But sometimes we teeter on the edge of a challenge, nervously asking, "Do you really mean it, Lord? Are you sure you can handle this one?"

Trusting our Father to catch us means we have to actually jump into life, not knowing exactly what will happen but believing every moment that he loves us and will see us safely through the adventure. As the old hymn says, we're "simply trusting day by day, simply trusting all the way."

In his book *Ruthless Trust,* Brennan Manning wrote about a brilliant student he had taught in seminary. Later the young man divided each year of his life into two parts. For six months of the year he lived as a hermit in a remote cabin in Tennessee. The rest of the year he traveled the country, preaching on behalf of a missionary outreach aimed at feeding the poor.

During a visit, Brennan asked the young man if he could define the Christian life in a single sentence.

"He didn't even blink before responding," Brennan wrote. He answered, "I can define it in a single word: *trust*."

My personal motto, "Whatever, Lord!" is simply the word *trust* translated into Geranium Lady language. Many times I have peered over the edge of a cliff of sorrow, staring at a dark, narrow valley of grief below, and said, "Lord, I don't think I can do this. Are you sure you can catch me? Are you really there? Are you really, really, *really* ready for this?"

And each time his promise echoes reassuringly in my spirit: "I will be with you always" (Matthew 28:20 NCV).

With those empowering words piercing through to the core of my being, I have stepped off the cliff and plunged into heartache—the deaths of two sons, the eleven-year estrangement from another son, and most recently, a terrifying experience with cancer. There is no way to describe the depth of anguish I felt in those situations. Yet there was something else in that turmoil, too: a sense of peace, knowing God would catch me and hold me tight, no matter what happened.

~ *Lord, you are the net beneath my tightrope, the lifeguard who saves me from the undertow, and the soothing breeze that dries my tears. I trust you, Lord! Amen.*

# You're Doing This for Your Father

## LUCI SWINDOLL

~

*Your attitude should be the same*
*as that of Christ Jesus. (Philippians 2:5)*

I'M SURROUNDED BY PAPERWORK. IT'S TAX TIME around here, and there are forms all over the place. I dropped by a friend's house this morning for coffee, and when I walked in the door she said, "Don't look in the kitchen . . . the counter's covered with tax papers. It's driving me crazy."

"Believe me, I know . . . I have the same thing at my house," I commiserated.

Who likes forms? Nobody. Somewhere on the outskirts of town pieces of paper are multiplying during the night, making little baby forms to come into our lives to strangle us. I'm convinced of it. As the rock musician Frank Zappa said in his autobiography, "It isn't necessary to imagine the world ending in fire or ice—there are two other possibilities: one is paperwork and the other, nostalgia."

I'll take nostalgia. I'd rather go to my grave from sentimental yearning than be eaten alive by an army of paperwork—the fire ants of the legal world.

A couple of weeks ago I was in the doctor's office (my first visit), and the nurse asked with a smile, "Would you mind filling these out first?" She handed me a clipboard laden with forms. Thank goodness I write fast, or I could have passed away before anybody knew my weight, Social Security number, mother's maiden name, or reason for being there.

I don't care what they're for—a doctor, a loan, a reimbursement, an adoption, a job, a new car, house, boat . . . whatever—nobody enjoys filling out forms. We just want them to go away.

One day when I was waiting in line to put a vacation stop on my mail delivery (had to pick up the form), I began analyzing the reasons I didn't want to be in that line. I came up with three.

First, and foremost—*forms take too much time*. Time is what I crave more than anything, more than money or energy. I fight to have more time and never seem to have enough.

Second—*forms require information not readily at hand*. I have to put down my pen, dig in my purse or a drawer, and look up the exact date of when I last had a mammogram or my long-forgotten home address of twenty years ago.

And third—*forms require data that isn't necessary*. Who cares that one of my siblings is left-handed or that my concern with risktaking is greater than my first cousin's? It makes no sense.

Having said all that, there's been only one time I had to fill out forms (for days, literally) that I'll never regret as long as I live. In looking back I realize those forms gave my father three years of life he wouldn't have had otherwise. I got him on Medicare.

You can spend months getting somebody on Medicare. And doing so necessitated my checking into his Social Security and insurance policies as well. *More* paperwork. I drove from building to building day after day after day, filling out reams of paper. Many a time I wanted to throw in the towel because the information requested seemed irrelevant, there were so many questions I couldn't answer, and . . . needless to say, it took *time*.

But here's what saved my sanity: I kept telling myself, "You're doing this for your father, Luci. Remember that. He can't get his health needs met unless he has the money, and he won't have the money unless somebody gets him on Medicare. You are that somebody! It's for him, not you. Now shut up and *write*. Just fill out the next form." And I'd dive in again.

Finally, the paperwork was done. I presented everything to the Medicare office where they inspected it carefully and assured me they had all the information they needed. In turn, they gave me an official card for Daddy. I took that to the nursing home where he lived and was told that my dad's medical bills would be paid each month.

I visited Daddy almost every day for three years, and when he died in March of 1980, I was so glad I had done the work that gave him financial solvency.

The only way to get through some things I'm required to do in life is to continually remind myself, "You're doing this for your Father, Luci." The apostle Paul said the same thing to the early Christians: "Whatever you do, work at it with all your heart, as working for the Lord, not for men" (Colossians 3:23).

*Whatever* you do?

Yes!

Even filling out *forms*?

Yup! *Whatever.*

Perhaps you're facing something today that is pure drudgery: meeting a deadline, losing weight, saving money, cleaning house, paying bills . . . Whatever it is, you're feeling "woe-is-me." I've been right where you are and understand the feeling. So does our heavenly Father.

More than likely, the drudgery isn't going to go away. But the bad attitude can. And who knows? Someday you may even find out why you had to go through it. Meanwhile, dive in and do whatever you have to do—do it as unto the Lord. Your reward is from him. That's what transforms drudgery into an adventure.

Well, almost!

~ *Lord, I'm so glad I don't have to fill out a form to get your attention. You know everything about me already. Whew! Help me to do whatever is in front of me today for you. Help me remember that it is you who sees, cares, listens, knows, and enables. You're the one I want to please! Amen.*

# Sin As Hope

## MARILYN MEBERG

~

*Fools mock at sin. (Proverbs 14:9 NASB)*

I'VE BEEN THINKING ABOUT SIN. IN FACT, I've been thinking about it a lot.

I read those two sentences to Luci, asking her if she thought they were a "reader turnoff."

"No, Marilyn . . . I'm preparing for some juicy confession you're about to make. Keep writing!"

Actually, I'm not about to make a confession, juicy or otherwise; but my sin ponderings have indeed been inspired lately by Barbara Brown Taylor's book *Speaking of Sin: The Lost Language of Salvation.* Taylor's premise is that certain words like *sin, damnation, repentance,* and *salvation* are rarely used anymore. The result? By not using a word like *sin,* we are in essence denying that we have sin. That means we lose the relief as well as the joy that comes with repentance and forgiveness. Moving from sin to forgiveness and a state of grace is the greatest adventure the spirit can experience, but the full impact cannot be experienced if we don't first acknowledge our sin.

The fact that "the *sin* word" is currently considered almost politically incorrect is in many ways understandable. The word has frequently been used in an abusive manner—a manner that gave no hope beyond the condition.

For example, I recall Mr. Dillston—an elderly, crabby man in one of the churches my dad pastored. Mr. Dillston's one-phrase evaluation for nearly everything and everyone was a hoarsely barked, "Gotta be sin there." As an eight-year-old who was easily spooked and overly conscientious, I avoided Mr. Dillston as much as possible. I often worried, *What does he know, and how does he know it?*

When my dog King died suddenly and mysteriously, Mr. Dillston shouted to me from the church steps, "Your dog's dead. Gotta be sin there." I didn't know if he was referring to my sin or King's. I also was mystified about how he knew my dog was dead; King had died only the day before Mr. Dillston's harsh pronouncement.

This was a story I had shared with Ken during the early stages of our courtship. Mr. Dillston's phrase became a part of our playful interaction throughout our marriage. "Had a bad board meeting, Ken. Gotta be sin there." "Ah, Marilyn, you have a sore throat and runny nose. Gotta be sin there."

One of my professors in college claimed he had not sinned in fifty years. We used to joke about that outside of class. "Hey, Tom . . . I haven't sinned in five minutes . . . whoops . . . there's that amply endowed girl with her too-tight cashmere sweater . . . never mind."

Abuse of the word *sin* and even confusion about what sin is can work to our disadvantage. *Sin* is a word we need to know; we need to use it at appropriate times because therein lies the hope. Hope of what? God's forgiveness and cleansing grace.

Just for the record, let's define *sin*. The dictionary says it's "a transgression of a religious or moral law." The theological definition is that "sin produces an estrangement from God as a result of breaking God's law." Here's where hope comes into play as we honestly face the fact that we have sinned. God provided a solution for sin and a way to no longer be estranged from him. It's called repentance. Scripture states that repentance should be accompanied by sorrow. "I will be sorry for my sin," says David in Psalm 38:18 KJV. Sorrow for sin is not a superficial "oops." Genuine repentance is a holy agony. But once authentic repentance occurs, we are forgiven. As if that weren't fantastic enough, God says he not only forgives the sin, but he forgets it. "I will forgive their iniquity, and their sin I will remember no more" (Jeremiah 31:34 NASB).

I think we're all pretty clear about murder, rape, robbery, and adultery as the "big sins" that for the most part belong to "them" . . . those "other" people. But what about those of us who may have a critical spirit and a biting tongue? Do we call that sin? What do we call it? Perhaps we say, "I speak my mind; not everyone likes that." Or, "Someone has to speak up against that choir director's flamboyant and distracting style of directing. He looks like a Ferris wheel!"

I don't know about you, but my tongue and spirit can be just as murderous as a terrorist attack; it's just on a smaller scale and doesn't make the six o'clock news. *Evil* is defined as "something that is a cause or source of suffering, injury, or destruction." Evil is sin. A critical spirit and a biting tongue can cause suffering and injury. Unless I choose to label my behavior as sin and relinquish the more comfortable label of "outspoken," I don't have the hope of forgiveness. But when I tell the truth about myself, repent, and receive forgiveness, I'm cleansed of the stain of sin.

What a relief . . . what a positive source of renewal the word *sin* can initiate. That grace process promises adventure for the soul every day. As a result I can dive into my life with new energy and fresh enthusiasm. I am a sinner, but I am a forgiven one!

So there, Mr. Dillston . . . what do you say to that?

~ *Lord, give me the courage to call my sin what it is. Amen.*

# Sloppy Agape

## PATSY CLAIRMONT

~

*The LORD will surely comfort Zion
and will look with compassion on all her ruins;
he will make her deserts like Eden,
her wastelands like the garden of the LORD.
Joy and gladness will be found in her. (Isaiah 51:3)*

MY FRIEND JANET GRANT OWNS A DOG named Murphy. Wait, let me try that again. Murphy, a dog, owns my friend Janet. There, that's more accurate.

Murphy is an Australian shepherd; actually, he's still a pup—a very determined, sanguine puppy. *Zealous* doesn't begin to describe his energy, which makes life adventurous for the Grants.

Janet and her hubby, Loch, were making a day trip to visit new friends and decided, at their friends' invitation, to bring Murphy along. They realized they would need to be vigilant lest their joyful live wire and his playful ways overwhelm the homeowners.

Murphy was on his best behavior, but it's difficult to squelch exuberance for long periods of time, and soon Murphy bounded into the living room to present his owners with a gift. Everyone tried not to overreact when they spotted an antique doll dangling from his toothy grin. Janet and Loch breathed a sigh of relief, as did the homeowners, when they were able to retrieve the treasure intact.

Then Murphy decided to be best friends with the home-owner's black Lab, Jill. Only problem was, Jill's friendship card was full, and she was not interested. Murphy's enthusiasm was not diminished. He would sidle up to Jill, who would growl her strong disapproval. Murphy would lay his paw over hers, which really ticked off Jill.

That's when it happened. Jill wasn't about to put up with this adolescent Casanova, especially on her home turf. She took the stance of a predator—front shoulders dropped, ears down. Then she let rip with her fiercest growl, and to drive home her intention to rearrange Murphy's anatomy, she bared her intimidating teeth.

Janet, Loch, and their friends were shocked at what happened next. Instead of backing away, Murphy bounded up into Jill's face. Oblivious to her disgust, Murphy began to lick her teeth. Yes, *her teeth*. Much to everyone's amazement, instead of ripping off Murphy's nose, Jill eased away, and while still not willing to be buddies, from that point on she tolerated Murphy's bubbly presence.

That story makes me giggle. Can't you just see it? Jill gives her best impression of a livid lunatic and receives in return sloppy *agape*.

I had that happen with my kids when they were young. I'd be in a snappy mood, growling around the house, when some-one would push me over the edge and I would have a little snarling fit. More than once after a teeth-baring episode, one of my sons would climb into my lap, kiss me, and nuzzle his little head up under my neck. Aww.

The part about Murphy's behavior I love best is his inextinguishable zeal for life and relationships. He just dived in headfirst.

Even though I'm impressed with the indomitable spirit of some, too much happy can be unnerving. Folks who force happy remind me of times when I've worn shoes a size too small and tried to walk as though they fit perfectly. It's so unnatural. But those whose joy is genuine and running over are compelling, right, Jill? Their gladness is an internal, eternal spring that draws people to its Source.

Mary Graham, president of Women of Faith, is that kind of gal. She's an example of compelling joy. She is wise, playful, generous, and relational. Everyone wants to be Mary's best friend, and, gratefully, the Lord has given her an expansive heart; she warmly embraces many. Mary's unassuming ways, her humorous tilt on life, and her commitment to God's truth are thoroughly enjoyable to behold.

Can you think of someone whose life exudes joy? As you think of him or her, what qualities do you see that you admire? Are those qualities a part of your character? Would you like them to be?

Joy is not a private-stock item reserved for the privileged; in fact, it's more like a community pool. All are invited. Dive in!

> Joy of heaven, to earth come down;
> Fix in us thy humble dwelling;
> All thy faithful mercies crown!

Jesus, thou art all compassion,
Pure, unbounded love thou art;
Visit us with thy salvation;
Enter every trembling heart.
                    —Charles Wesley

~ *Dear Lord, we invite you to enter our trembling hearts. This adventure called life can be intimidating at times, but when we are exuberant in you we can face any challenge with confidence— even joy. Amen.*

# Freedom Behind Bars

## SHEILA WALSH

~

*How beautiful on the mountains are the feet of those who bring good
news, who proclaim peace, who bring good tidings, who proclaim
salvation, who say to Zion, "Your God reigns!" (Isaiah 52:7)*

CINDY HAS BEEN ONE OF MY DEAREST
friends for more than fifteen years. We are the same age, and
our birthdays are only a couple of weeks apart. Barry and
Christian love her, too. She is very much part of our family.

I met Cindy when she was the production coordinator on
one of my albums and immediately clicked with her crazy
sense of humor and her love for God. She has been involved
in the Christian music arena for years, working with song-
writers and producers, giving wings to the gifts and talents of
others. But four years ago she branched out in an unusual way.

Her pastor announced to his congregation one Sunday
morning that the church had received a request from the
Tennessee Prison for Women. They were looking for someone to lead a Bible study on Sunday evenings at the prison
chapel. Cindy had never had any interest in that kind of
work, but as she listened to the request, God began to
prompt her to respond to this opportunity to serve him. She
took the plunge, having no idea what to expect or how to

relate to women behind bars. What she discovered has changed her life.

A few weeks ago Cindy and her mom (sweet Grandma Lois to Christian) were at our house for supper. After dinner we were talking about her work at the prison. As she related her experience, Cindy's eyes sparkled with the passion of someone who has taken a risk, dived into a new venture, and discovered a priceless pearl.

"I get there about five-thirty every Sunday night," she told us. "The women come to Freedom Chapel at six. We have a time of worship and then move into our Bible study. I love these women. I love showing up in their lives. Sunday night has become the highlight of my week. I never dreamed that I would have so much in common with women serving time or find such incredible joy in seeing God transform their lives."

The women have come to so love and trust Cindy that if she has to miss a Sunday night for any reason, they expect her to provide a written excuse!

When I first met Cindy I would never have imagined her doing this kind of work. Now she is forty-six and single. She could sit at home on a Sunday night watching TV, or show up at every Bible study in town looking for "Mr. Right," but instead she gives her time and heart away to bring good news to those whose lives have taken unexpected turns. The amazing thing is that in the midst of being stretched in uncomfortable ways, she has found a passion and joy in life that had not been there before. If I ask her how her job is going, she'll give me a couple of sentences about her latest project; but if I ask her about the Tennessee Prison for Women, I'd better sit down with a cup of coffee because we'll be there for a while!

God gives each of us different opportunities to be the bearers of his good news. For some it might be in a prison or a hospital, a small neighborhood Bible study, or a one-on-one friendship with someone who has never met Christ. It's a scary thing to take the plunge and reach out, but it's a wonderful adventure. Cindy could have gone to the prison once and told the women that they needed Jesus, offered the prayer of salvation, and gone back to her comfortable life. Instead, she has shown up at Freedom Chapel every week for four years, bringing the fragrance of Christ to those who take some time to trust.

How long has it been since you dived into unfamiliar waters? Take the plunge! It's an exhilarating way to live.

~ *Father, I ask you to show me ways to be your good news in the life of someone who has no idea that you love her. In Jesus' name, amen.*

# Part 6

~

## Ain't No Mountain High Enough:

### Dare to Dream and Discover

# Gossamer Wings

## Patsy Clairmont

~

*Come, let us go up to the mountain of the LORD. (Micah 4:2)*

DID YOU KNOW THAT TENS OF MILLIONS OF monarch butterflies travel six thousand miles from Latin America to arrive in the United States each spring? Talk about adventuresome! Imagine that liftoff.

Monarchs have been tracked flying as far as seventy miles a day. That's quite miraculous when you consider their delicate body design, minute weight, and gossamer wings. Even a gentle puff of wind could sideswipe a butterfly; yet these tenacious beauties persist in their trek.

(By the way, I'm told their energy supply comes from fat stored up in their stomachs. Hmm, this could be the perfect response to inquiring relatives or friends regarding whether we've gained weight. "Why, no, darlings, it's just fuel for the journey, but thank you for asking.")

I, like the butterfly, can easily be blown off course. Just walking from my living room to the bedroom can be a long hike as I sidestep to straighten the slipcover on a chair, adjust a crooked picture, answer the doorbell, sort through the mail, and gather up the strewn newspaper. By the time I amble into the bedroom, I can't remember why I thought I wanted to be there. Unlike the monarch, I'm not as quick to get back on course.

I've found staying on course—whether you're a tissue-paper butterfly or an unfocused woman—is important if one is to reach her destination and see her dreams come true. When I was a child, I dreamed of being a writer. Well-placed words were pleasing to my soul. Yet when I entered high school, my rebellious attitudes squelched my vision for the future and left me full of myself. Eventually, I learned that too much self leaves one with an acidic palate. Yikes, somebody pass the Zantac!

Decades later this erratic journeyer found the right airstream and fluttered back on course. But I had to wade through my rebellion, a series of poor choices, my emotional muddle, and deep feelings of inadequacy before I recaptured direction for my life.

Every feeble step in the right direction felt like trying to scale a steep, rocky incline. I'd take a few shaky steps and fall down or slip and lose ground. Bloody knees, bruised shins, and scraped arms often slowed my progress. Yet I knew if I didn't climb the mountain, I wouldn't see the view with its vistas of hope.

When I was invited to write my first book, I thought I had reached the mountaintop. But then I realized that, while I was on a high ledge, the summit was looming above. I still had to create a manuscript. From scratch! Me, who "earned" D's in high school English classes; me, who in the eleventh grade dropped out of school.

I'm grateful I was assigned an editor who became a valued

guide and dear friend. I wrote each chapter over and over according to my editor's red-marked expertise. My high school teachers would have been overjoyed to see I was finally paying my dues.

Looking back on the years of recovery before my writing dream came true, I can now say that scaling the rugged terrain was worth the cost. I've even learned to enjoy homework. Don't tell my teachers.

As I consider how off-course I had veered and how God's mercy brought me back to my intended flight pattern, my mind meanders back to the monarch. It amazes me that an insect we could tuck into a pocket speaks eloquently to us of beauty, grace, and endurance—a visual aid on the importance of finishing the race set before us. If a bug the weight of a breath can cover thousands of miles in its six to nine months of life, what were we created to accomplish? Why, our potential is endless. So haul out your hiking boots and hook your climbing rope to the Rock.

~ *Jesus, Rock of our faith, guide us up the mountains you've placed in the terrain of our lives. Give us the footholds we need to conquer the steep inclines. Thank you that you will tend to our bruised hearts, our scarred pasts, and our limited vision. And when we think we can't go on, will you give us gossamer wings to lift us above our fears? We want to catch the air currents that contain the dreams you have for us. Amen.*

# As the World Talks

LUCI SWINDOLL

~

*Therefore go and make disciples of all nations, baptizing them in the name of the Father and of the Son and of the Holy Spirit, and teaching them to obey everything I have commanded you. And surely I am with you always, to the very end of the age. (Matthew 28:19–20)*

WHEN I WAS ABOUT TEN YEARS OLD I REmember being in a post office one day with my father. On the wall was a framed poster about World War II—there was a young military man in a well-pressed uniform, saluting. Beneath him were these words:

JOIN THE ARMY AND SEE THE WORLD.

I said to Daddy, "I want to do that."

"You want to join the army?"

"No, I want to see the world."

That little exchange occurred in the early forties, but for some reason I remember it. I've always been fascinated by the world. Geography. Cultures. Peoples. Languages. Typography. Maps. As a child it never occurred to me I'd get to see as much of the planet as I have, but I certainly knew I wanted to.

The first "frivolous gadget" (Mother's words) I bought after getting a little job was a world globe. It satisfied a curiosity in me that I couldn't quite define. I'd look at it, spin it, read stories about Europe or South America or Africa, and dream of going there one day to explore and discover.

Now, many years later, I have an enormous, sophisticated globe that's on a stand, with wheels on the bottom so I can roll it anywhere in the house. A friend from northern California was here several months ago and we moved it into the living room and talked travel for three hours, pointing out various places we've been or plan to go. He's traveled in every continent, and because I was seeing each place through Kurt's eyes, I felt I had actually taken a trip around the world when the evening ended.

My most recent "globe mania" acquisition is a *GeoSafari*. A home-school teacher had bought one for her boys and when she told me about it I said, "I have to have that"— so she sent me one. Guess what—it talks! There are little buttons on the base, and when they're pushed the globe asks questions . . . true or false and multiple-choice, about all kinds of geographical topics. It is now my favorite toy. Only, I don't really consider it a toy. I consider it a treasure because it gives me a chance to learn lots of new things in a fun way, and it dares me to keep my little-girl dreams to see the world alive as long as I'm on Earth.

I'm pleased and comforted to know that God, too, is interested in the world.

He founded the world and all that's in it—Psalm 89:11.

He's Lord of the world—Zechariah 6:5.

He loves the world—John 3:16.

His Son took away the sin of the world—John 1:29.

He gives life to the world—John 6:33.

And, one of the greatest messages in Scripture is that God invites his followers to go all over the world, telling people about him (see Mark 16:15).

In April 2000, Women of Faith had the opportunity to be in India on a mission trip with World Vision, the relief organization that gives aid to underprivileged families worldwide. In the city of Chennai we visited a care center for women where HIV/AIDS victims are being treated, primarily through the efforts of a thirty-four-year-old Indian psychiatrist who is a Christian. In flawless English, Dr. Punitha told us how excited the women were that we were coming.

"We rarely have anybody come from the other side of the world. What a treat this is for us. Thank you."

It was our privilege to hear the women's testimonies, visit with them, and enjoy their singing and dancing as we sat around the room, a mesmerized audience.

While in India we also had a chance to meet three lovely young women (all in their twenties) who have been sponsored since childhood by World Vision donors. Their names are Pamela, Mitcy, and Michelle. They've known each other since they were little girls and are now working on advanced studies at the university. We had dinner with them one evening.

Thelma Wells asked them what they were most grateful for from World Vision. (A great question.) Pamela answered for the whole group: "Before World Vision came to India we were in darkness. We had no hope, no light." Then she pointed to a candle on the table and said, "It was like that candle before it was lit . . . just there, but not doing that for which it was made. World Vision came to India and 'lit the candle.'" What a marvelous testimony for the work of World Vision!

I've been thinking, since I got my *GeoSafari* globe . . . wouldn't it be informative and inspiring if we could punch a button on its base and hear various persons around the world tell us about those who came from faraway lands and introduced them to the Savior? I'm sure we'd hear wonderful stories of sacrifice and love.

For those who take the words of Jesus literally and go to other nations with the message of good news, I believe there are unique and unparalleled blessings. I have friends in Italy, Greece, Argentina, Ghana, and India who would never have met Jesus Christ personally had someone from another country not gone there and told them about God's incomparable gift of grace.

We've been invited to see the world with an eternal mission in mind. The adventure is ours for the daring.

*⌁ Heavenly Father, in Jesus' name I pray you will continue to open doors all over the world for the good news of eternal life to go forth. And, Lord, make me a part of that great work in whatever way you choose. Amen.*

# The Powerful Fragrance of Love

## SHEILA WALSH

~

*But thanks be to God, who always leads us in*
*triumphal procession in Christ and through us*
*spreads everywhere the fragrance of the knowledge of him.*
*(2 Corinthians 2:14)*

A FRIEND SENT ME A STORY THIS WEEK THAT beautifully illustrates the potential each one of us has to powerfully impact a life that we are brought into contact with. To protect her privacy I'll change the names, but the story is about a teacher I'll call Mrs. Brown.

One of Mrs. Brown's fifth-grade students was a little boy named Sam. The teacher quickly noticed that Sam didn't play well with the other children, that he performed poorly in his studies, and that his clothes were messy and his personal hygiene poor. She found herself actually taking delight in marking his papers with a broad red pen, making bold X's and then that devastating F at the top.

The school required teachers to review each child's past records, and Mrs. Brown put Sam's off until last. When she finally reviewed his file, she was shocked by the story it told. It seemed to be describing a different child.

"Sam is a bright child with a ready laugh. He does his work

neatly and has good manners. He is a joy to be around," Sam's first-grade teacher wrote.

His second-grade teacher reported, "Sam is an excellent student, well liked by his classmates, but he is troubled because his mother has a terminal illness and life at home must be a struggle."

When Sam reached third grade, his teacher warned, "His mother's death has been hard on him. He tries to do his best, but his father doesn't show much interest and his home life will soon affect him if some steps aren't taken."

His fourth-grade teacher said, "Sam is withdrawn and doesn't show much interest in school. He doesn't have many friends, and he sometimes sleeps in class."

Mrs. Brown, seeing the larger picture, was ashamed of her attitude toward this broken boy. Her empathy for him was further heightened when her students brought their Christmas presents for her that year, wrapped in beautiful ribbons and bright paper—except for Sam's, which was wrapped in a brown-paper grocery bag. Some of the children started to laugh when she opened his gift and found a rhinestone bracelet with some of the stones missing, and a bottle that was one-quarter full of perfume. But she put the bracelet on and dabbed some of the perfume on her wrist. Sam stayed after school that day just long enough to say, "Mrs. Brown, today you smelled just like my mother used to."

After the students left, she cried for an hour. She now says that on that day she quit teaching reading, writing, and arithmetic and began teaching children, paying particular attention to Sam. As she worked with him, his mind seemed to come alive. The more she encouraged him, the faster he responded. By the end of the year, he had become one of the most accomplished children in the class. A year later, she found a note from Sam under her classroom door, telling her that she was the best teacher he'd ever had.

Six years later she received another note. Sam wrote that he had finished high school, third in his class, and she was still the best teacher he had had in his whole life. Four years after that, she got another letter, saying that while things had been tough at times, he'd stayed in school, had stuck with it, and would soon graduate from college with top honors. He assured Mrs. Brown that she was still the best and favorite teacher he had ever had. Four more years passed and another letter came. This time he explained that after he had achieved his bachelor's degree, he decided to go a little further. The letter simply stated that she was still the best and favorite teacher he'd ever had. But now his name was a little longer. The letter was signed, *Sam F. Stone, M.D.*

That spring brought yet another letter. Sam said he'd met a girl and was going to be married. He explained that his father had died a couple of years ago, and he was wondering if Mrs. Brown might agree to sit in the place at the wedding that was usually reserved for the mother of the groom. She accepted his invitation and wore the bracelet with the missing rhinestones. She also made sure she was wearing the perfume that reminded Sam of his mother. They hugged each other, and Dr. Stone whispered in Mrs. Brown's ear, "Thank you for believing in me. Thank you so much for making me feel important and showing me that I could make a difference."

Mrs. Brown, with tears in her eyes, whispered back, "Sam, you have it all wrong. You were the one who taught me that I could make a difference. I didn't know how to teach until I met you."

*~ Father, I ask that today you will give me your eyes to see, your ears to hear, and your heart to love. May the fragrance of your Son, Jesus, be so sweet in me that other people will dare to dream that they can be all you've created them to be. Amen.*

# Aunt Crazy's Recovery

## Thelma Wells

~

*The people went out to see what had happened;*
*and they came to Jesus, and found the man from whom*
*the demons had gone out, sitting down at the feet of Jesus,*
*clothed and in his right mind. (Luke 8:35 NASB)*

WE HAD A BIG MAILING PROJECT WITH A deadline to meet. So I asked my assistant at A Woman of God Ministries if she knew someone who could help stuff, seal, and sort two thousand pieces of mail. After thinking for a while Pat suggested her lifelong friend and relative by marriage. Sure, that was fine with me. If the woman could breathe, see, stuff, and lick, she was in.

My assistant cautioned me, however, that her in-law had been under a psychiatrist's care for years and had several mental challenges. With some hesitance, I consented. Anyway, she was going to be working with Pat, not me. If things got too unbearable, I'd just leave the office.

Sure enough, the following day, in walked Pat and her relative. The woman sat silently but worked swiftly to get those letters out. She worked so fast that I wondered, "Is she real or is she a robot?" We beat our deadline for mailing the letters by one day.

After we had finished with the letters, the robot-woman told me she just needed to get out of the house. She asked if she could keep working for me. As a master delegator, I can always find something for someone to do to keep them occupied. My husband, the business manager of the ministry, looked at the budget and determined that we could offer her part-time work. I was not surprised when she accepted.

One day she came into my office and told me several reasons why she enjoyed coming to work. A very important reason, she confided, was that I have gospel music playing most of the time. This particular week I didn't have the music on because I was working on a writing deadline and I wanted it quiet. She asked me why the music was not playing, adding, "I need that music on because it helps me keep my mind on where the Lord has brought me, and I feel like he's sitting beside me. Since I've been coming here, I'm beginning to feel alive again. Please keep the music playing. I enjoy hearing you chime in and sing a verse or chorus. You just don't know what this means to me."

She was right! I didn't realize what the music meant to her. I only know what it does for me.

It's been nearly seven years since the mail-deadline day, and that dear woman is still with me. She had a lot of fears and hang-ups when she came. She couldn't stand crowds. Now she travels with me at least twenty-seven times a year and mans my product table at the Women of Faith conferences that draw from nine to twenty thousand women at a time. She couldn't stand to fly. Now every time a plane is ready to take off to where we need to go, she's one of the first in line to board the aircraft. She used to wear dark, drab clothes. Check her out now in her bright pinks, purples, reds, greens, and blues. Not only are her clothes colorful, but they also have "stuff" on them—sequins, appliqués, ribbons, the works. She's become a fashion plate.

The thing she feared most was water. She vowed to never participate in any water excursion deeper than a half-full bathtub. What did she do year before last? She went on an eight-day Caribbean cruise with Women of Faith. But that's not the kicker. She accompanied us to Niagara Falls, where she embarked on the *Maid of the Mist* and rode the rapids down the river to the Falls. As the ride was ending I noticed her crying. *Oh, dear, she's losing it!* I thought. I started to move toward her, but she told me in no uncertain terms, "No, I'm fine! I don't need you!" Well, excuse me. I stayed where I was.

When we got off the boat, she was still crying. But there was a sweetness and calmness in her tears that was soothing. When Pat and I asked her what happened, she told us that she felt someone hug her and she thought it was one of us. But nobody was standing by her. She knew it was the touch of God, in the form of the Holy Spirit, comforting her and letting her know that she was delivered from her debilitating terror. We all rejoiced as she told everybody in our group what had happened to her.

"Aunt Crazy" was what her family called her when she came to work at A Woman of God Ministries. They didn't mean any harm; that was their affectionate nickname for the lady they knew who'd had mental problems for longer than some of them had been alive. Her name is not Aunt Crazy anymore. Her sons call her Mama. Her grandchildren call her Nana. Her nieces and nephews call her Aunt Karole. The folks at her church call her Mrs. Jones. In the office we think of her as Blessed.

Karole didn't know that she was about to scale a mountain when she came to help stuff and lick two thousand envelopes. But she had the presence of mind to know that something good was happening to her, and she was willing to keep taking the next step in front of her. Because she has faced her fears head-on, she can say from experience, "Ain't no mountain high enough to keep me from you, Jesus!"

*~ Sweet Holy Spirit, please wrap your loving arms around all of us and let us feel the deliverance of your presence and protection. Help us to realize that tight, dark corners are not your will for our lives. You have placed us on the path of adventure, and we want to follow your lead all the way. Amen.*

# The Two Most Wonderful Words

### Barbara Johnson

~

*But if we confess our sins, he will forgive our sins,*
*because we can trust God to do what is right.*
*He will cleanse us from all the wrongs we have done.*
*(1 John 1:9 NCV)*

RECENTLY I HEARD BILLY GRAHAM SAY that Mark Twain, when he was asked what were the most wonderful words in the English language, answered immediately, "Not guilty!"

How blessed we are as we skip, trudge, or stumble along life's journey to have that get-out-of-jail-free card in 1 John 1:9. As Christians, we are *forgiven*. No matter what mistakes we've made or misadventures we've had or what trouble we've stirred up along the way, if we have confessed our sins to God and asked for his forgiveness—we're *not guilty*!

If there's anyone who needs to hear that message again and again it's parents, especially parents of wayward children. Hundreds of these parents have called me after learning their child is homosexual or is causing them anguish in some other way. They say, "Barb, I don't know what I did to cause my child to turn out this way, but it must be my fault. Otherwise, why would I feel such guilt?"

I remind them of the late Erma Bombeck's famous line: Guilt is the gift that keeps on giving. And I can personally vouch for Erma's wisdom! There are times when feelings of appropriate guilt can be a good thing. They can convince us of our mistakes and push us toward asking forgiveness, both from the person we wronged and from God. But once that's done, we need to leave that problem behind us and move on up the mountain! Until we do, we're carrying a backpack full of heavy, worthless rocks—a foolish, unnecessary burden—as we struggle to climb life's steep, narrow footpath.

I used to have a little can of stuff labeled "1 John 1:9— Spray Away Guilt." It was some goofy room deodorizer, but the clever little visual aid carried a big wallop, and I loved showing it whenever I spoke to groups of parents. Just as quickly as a room deodorizer removes foul smells from a room, God's wonderful promise erases the sins from our lives. We confess our sins to him, ask his forgiveness, and *poof!* they're gone. It seems so easy. Yet Jesus paid a terrible price for our sins. And when we fail to claim the forgiveness his death offered us, when we continue to feel guilty for mistakes we've confessed and been forgiven for, we're rejecting the loving sacrifice he made for us.

When God forgives us, our transgressions are cast into the sea of God's forgetfulness, and he remembers them no more (see Hebrews 8:12). Someone said that when God throws our sins into the bottom of the ocean, we should resist the urge to get out a fishing pole and dredge them up again! I like to say the one thing God cannot do is see our sins when they're covered by Christ's blood. And if *he* doesn't remember them, then why should they keep tormenting *us*?

Whenever you notice the old guilt feelings bubbling up within you, try to remember that it's not God reviving them within your mind. Rather, it's a scheme of the devil, trying to take your focus away from God and the potential he's created in you, as a forgiven and victorious woman, to scale even the highest "mountains" on your horizon.

Think of the courtroom scene depicted in so many movies and television shows. The jury solemnly files into the room, the judge sits ready to pronounce sentence, the accused person stands nervously before the court awaiting the reading of the verdict. When the next words are "Not guilty," the defendant collapses in relief or erupts in exuberant joy. It's as if the chains of bondage are broken, and the long-suffering captive is set free.

We can have that same joyful feeling as we live each day, knowing we've been forgiven by God. Someone once observed that there is no pillow so soft as a clear conscience. That's the gift God gives us when we stand before him, humbly ask his forgiveness, and then hear those wonderful words: *not guilty*.

Sleep well!

~ *Dear Jesus, you committed no sin and paid the ultimate price for all sinners. Thank you for cleansing me from the mistakes that threatened to stain my life. Help me to live each day fully aware of the gift of forgiveness you have given me. I choose to put down my backpack of "guilt rocks" right now and travel on up the mountain, free from the heavy burden. Amen.*

# Heavenly Signs

## MARILYN MEBERG

~

*Rescue the weak and needy. (Psalm 82:4)*

SKYWRITER JERRY STEVENS SEES HIMSELF as an evangelist for people looking for heavenly signs. In an interview with the *Palm Beach Post* he said, "You can't imagine what it's like when you're feeling low, wondering if God is listening to your prayers, and then you walk out of your house and up above in big letters right over you there's 'God Loves You.'" I can well imagine how that experience would give people an unexpected perk.

We all experience humdrum times when we go through the day's events with a "same-ol', same-ol'" mind-set.

"Where's the variety . . . where's the adventure?" we mutter to ourselves.

A biblical event that throws my imagination into gear is wondering if Moses was having one of those ho-hum days tending sheep, kicking sand, and then, without warning, there's this bush! The bush is on fire—and if that were not sufficiently unsettling, it talks.

I wonder how it went between Moses and Mrs. Moses when he wandered into the tent that evening. "How was your day?" asks Mrs. Moses. "Well, you're going to find this hard to believe, but I had an incredible conversation with a bush." *Uh huh.*

Few of us have the adventure of a burning bush experience, and if we did we'd probably keep quiet about it. Who would believe it? But there are various occasions when God still does the unexpected and dramatic. I experienced one of those occasions in the wee hours of March 7, 2000. I've decided not to keep quiet about it.

I didn't see a bush burning or hear one talk, but I feel certain that I had an encounter with the living God nevertheless. I've written before about the serious health battle I had with silicone toxicity four years ago. Several doctors advised me to drop off the Women of Faith speaking team since I didn't even have the stamina to walk to the mailbox, much less get to an airport. Since I'd lost nearly 70 percent of my hair and forty pounds, I figured I wouldn't be much of a visual draw no matter how I got to the airport. I settled in to the expectation that I'd be an unattractive invalid the rest of my life.

As I lay awake at 2:00 A.M. that spring morning (sleeplessness was common in my bout with toxicity), I was talking to God. I had the audacity to ask him for a tangible touch, an unmistakable awareness of his presence. Though I was weak as well as discouraged, it really isn't "my style" to pray for a God-manifestation. But I did—and he did!

I don't know what I expected, exactly: some comforting touch of a gentle Jesus who carried lambs who couldn't walk. Instead, my mind was suddenly abuzz with scripture after scripture that describes the awesome might and power of God. I was reminded that Deuteronomy continually describes him as a "devouring fire" and one committed to driving out our enemies. It was as though my spiritual eyes were "seeing" him driving out the enemy poisoning my body in those very moments. I was not immediately made whole, but I knew deep within my spirit that God intended for me to "take up my pallet and walk."

Several days later I boarded a plane for my first conference of the year. I went in a wheelchair, but gradually my health returned. Now, nearly four years later, I'm annoyingly energetic, have more hair than I need, and more pounds than my clothes seem able to accommodate.

Why do I share this very personal experience with you in a book whose subject is adventure? I do it because I want to encourage you to dare to believe that God is a God who gladly manifests his nature in ways that stretch our too-small ideas of him. He is poised to show us *all* of who he is, if we but open our minds and our spiritual eyes. He is a God who provides incredible adventure for our spirits.

So be on the alert. Dare to believe. Adventure from God may come in the middle of the night or from unexpected handwriting in the sky.

⁓ *Lord God Almighty, your power is ferocious; your love is constant. Thank you for both. Amen.*

# Press On!

## LUCI SWINDOLL

~

*"Age should speak; advanced years should teach wisdom."*
*But it is the spirit in a man, the breath of the Almighty,*
*that gives him understanding. (Job 32:7–8)*

WASN'T GEORGE BURNS OVER ONE HUNDRED
years old when he died? I loved that guy and found his philosophy of life invigorating at any age, but especially as he got older. A few of his homilies carry just the right twist to give me a chuckle. Ol' George said you know you're getting older when—

The parts of your body that have arthritis are the parts that feel the best.

Your knees buckle but your belt won't.

Your favorite section of the newspaper is "25 Years Ago Today."

Believe me, I've experienced every one of those signs of aging and many more I can't remember because, as you know, the mind is the first to go. Therefore, since my mind is on its way to the boneyard anyway, I'm determined to keep it as sharp as possible for as long as possible.

An example of one who never grew old (even in her eighties) was Edith Fleeman. Dear little darling, shy Edith Fleeman.

What a woman. About as big as a minute, she raced around through life doing good deeds for others, never complaining about her own burdens or problems. She inspired me on countless occasions when I watched her respond to bad news or ill health or family concerns, although she never knew I was taking mental notes.

Her daughter, Doris, has been a dear friend of mine for forty years, and together we used to marvel at her mother's ability to beat the odds with her incomparable, positive attitude. She simply would not be defeated.

There was the time she went to the doctor and learned she needed a hysterectomy, but rather than *bother* the family, she took matters into her own hands and called the hospital to set up her admission and surgery date. When the rest of us found out, we were stunned that it was practically over before we knew what happened. She was the model patient, never griping about anything that came her way. We used to go see her just to cheer ourselves up.

As Mrs. Fleeman neared the end of her life, her eyesight became so impaired she was confined to her home. Having lived there almost half a century, she had memorized the location of every room, of course . . . doorway, appliance, fixture, and piece of furniture . . . and could zip through the place at top speed. Doris and I used to whisper to each other, "We ought to race the woman to the kitchen because I *know for sure* we'd lose." Mrs. Fleeman, who heard *everything*, would just laugh and dare us to follow through.

But here's my favorite story about this wonderful little lady: When she was close to ninety, completely blind in one eye with very little vision left in the other, I asked her what she wanted for her birthday. Without hesitation she said, "I want a copy of that book by Aleksandr Solzhenitsyn, *The Gulag Archipelago*. I've wanted to read it and have never had the time. Just a paperback would be great."

Well. I have to tell you I thought this request was way too ambitious. This sweet old woman would *never* read the *Gulag*, even if she had fifty years yet to live. There was no way. First of all, it's a million pages long; second, one of her eyes was blind and the other impaired; third, she was too weak to hold it in her hands. But not wanting to disappoint her, I asked Doris what she thought I should do.

"Oh, Mother would love that, Luci," she said, "and I think she'd probably figure out a way to read it. She's pretty remarkable. Why don't you give it to her and see what happens."

When I first gave her the book, all gift-wrapped in bright paper, she opened it, smiled, and said how pleased she was, thanking me warmly. Then, without hesitation, she cut it in half. As the weeks passed she held half the book at a time in one hand and a magnifying glass in the other and finished the entire volume. "It's one of the finest works of literature I've ever read," she pronounced. She *loved* it.

And . . . (this is my favorite part) not only did Mrs. Fleeman read *The Gulag Archipelago*, but afterward she gave me the most well-expressed, brilliantly thought-out, cogent book report I've ever heard.

Mrs. Fleeman, who has been dead many, many years, will never know what a light she is to me as I peer down the dark, uncertain path of aging. She is a symbol for accomplishing anything at any age if one wants to bad enough. I've thought of her fireball spirit many times as I've considered the flagging debilitations that may accompany my own aging process. Edith Fleeman carries the torch for me, leading the way to glory. She's up there with the Lord, and when I see her someday I'm going to thank her for being my guide. She chose to live fully to the very end. She stayed alert and alive and interested in everything. Who doesn't admire that?

I had the opportunity last spring to go dogsledding on a glacier with a group from the Women of Faith Alaskan cruise. On our particular excursion there was a ninety-three-year-old woman. I marveled at her adventuresome, never-say-die spirit. After we got back to the ship I asked if she had fun. "One of the best things I ever did," she said with a twinkle in her eye. "I loved every minute." I thought of Mrs. Fleeman, my spirited role model. She would have loved it, too.

Everybody admires people who don't give up. It's what the apostle Paul was speaking of in Philippians 3:12 when he said, "I press on to take hold of that for which Christ Jesus took hold of me."

Make up your mind today that you're going to do something to help yourself stay young as long as possible—laugh more, start swimming, fly a kite, take up painting, plant a garden, read a big fat book. If it's too heavy to hold, cut it in half and read to your heart's content. Press on!

~ *Help me, Father, to face the future with joy and readiness and a sense of adventure. And keep me from being a crotchety old woman. Help me to keep pressing on. Amen.*

# No Matter What

## Barbara Johnson

~

*Though he slay me, yet will I trust in him. (Job 13:15 KJV)*

DRIVING HOME FROM THE GROCERY STORE, I stopped to let a fire truck roar past me, its siren blasting and lights flashing. *Hmmm,* I thought, *it seems to be heading toward my part of town.* Then, as I drove nearer, I noticed smoke billowing upward from the direction of my neighborhood. By the time I'd turned onto our street, which was lined with fire trucks and other emergency vehicles, my heart was pounding. The smoke was coming from a house that seemed to be close to ours . . . or maybe, oh no! It *was* our house that was burning!

I had been gone only about thirty minutes. The boys were teenagers then, and they were happily playing in the swimming pool, so while I was worried about them I assumed they were safe. But I panicked when I thought about Bill. This was a few months after his terrible car accident, and I had left him in the back bedroom so that the boys' antics wouldn't disturb his rest. Suffering from multiple broken bones, he was confined to a body cast and unable to get up.

My heart was in my throat as I braked the car to a screeching halt as close to the house as I could get. By then I could see tiny fingers of flame shooting out from under the roof of the porch. The fire was almost out, but most of the house was filled with smoke. Quickly I ascertained that the boys were all right, but they all seemed to be in shock, dumbstruck that the house had almost burned down.

Bill was nowhere in sight.

Frantically, I led a couple of the firefighters around to the back of the house. They hurried through the back door, ran to the back bedroom, burst open the door—and found Bill placidly lying there in bed, watching television. He was completely unaware of all the excitement that had engulfed the rest of us because, being in the back of the house, he hadn't heard all the commotion. His injuries in the wreck had completely destroyed his sense of smell, so he was also completely oblivious to the smoke that filled the house that day—and for many days to come. In fact, he was so out of it most of the time during that long, slow recovery that today he doesn't remember that terrifying afternoon at all.

Later that evening I stood there in my house—dripping with water from the firefighters' hoses and reeking with the stench of smoke—and thanked God that my family and my home had survived this day. Insurance would cover the fire and smoke damage, and my four boys and my husband were uninjured. I thought then, after having endured the awful months following the accident and the near loss of my home and family, that surely I had been tested enough and deemed loyal to God. Surely nothing else would happen to us, I thought.

But there was something else more solid in those thankful musings. By having survived these tragedies with my faith intact, I knew that no matter what else *did* happen, God would be with me through any difficulties that occurred. He had proved that fact. He had been with me through these dark hours, and I knew *from experience* that he would be with me for whatever was to come. I trusted him never to forsake me.

And sure enough, many more painful times did lie ahead of me—pitch-dark hours when two of our sons would die, a third son would disappear from our lives for eleven years, and later, when cancer would put the happy "busyness" of my life on indefinite hold. There were times during those challenging, heartbreaking experiences when I described myself as feeling like nothing, like a zero with the rim rubbed out. And yet even in that great void, God was present.

Job said, "Though he slay me, yet will I trust in him." And every day of my life, I echo Job's words and whisper a fervent *Amen!*

～ *Dear Jesus, I trust that the plan you have for my life will bring me ever closer to you. Because you have proved yourself faithful time and again, I will continue to move on and up in faith till I see your dear face. Amen.*

# Rocky Faith

PATSY CLAIRMONT

~

*Let us fix our eyes on Jesus, the author and perfecter of our faith,*
*who for the joy set before him endured the cross,*
*scorning its shame, and sat down at the right hand*
*of the throne of God. (Hebrews 12:2)*

FOR SEVERAL MONTHS EACH WINTER I LIVE surrounded by mountains in the California desert. In fact, I live in a basin. To me, that sounds as if, at any minute, someone could turn on a spigot, and I could be swirled into oblivion.

Funny thought, huh. Not ha-ha funny, but strange funny, which is why I have to continually take my thought patterns to the Lord. Lately, I've been thinking about faith . . .

At times, I've felt as if faith were a mountain looming above me, just like the mountains around our basin, and I'm a tiny mustard granule down below. I know Scripture says that if we have faith as small as a mustard seed and say to the mountain, "Move," it will; but I'm just describing how I sometimes feel.

An understanding of faith can be as difficult for me to embrace as if it were, say, Mount Everest. Oh, I believe in faith, but I don't always have the faith to believe, especially for the biggies like world hunger or world peace. Who am I kidding?

Why, sometimes I have trouble believing that my cranky neighbor will ever be saved or that my own bad attitudes will ever be properly adjusted. Ever feel that way? That's when I know I need to rely on the Lord more than ever.

Here's something else about faith I've noted: I've seen faith-filled folks live in perilous places and thrive. Likewise, I've seen faith-filled folks live in times of plenty and become spiritually emaciated. Do you think that means faith flourishes in the midst of hardships?

I guess, if we examined the lives of Joseph, Daniel, and Paul, we would see that their difficult circumstances certainly honed their faith. Or what about Hagar, who found her faith in her hardship; or Naomi, who had her flickering faith rekindled as she worked through her family's death; or the woman caught in adultery, whose faith was birthed in her humiliation?

We saw faith mount up in our nation after the terrorists' attack on September 11, 2001. Suddenly it was politically polite to speak of God and prayer. I liked that a lot. The evil attack I despised, but the divine interlude our country experienced was heartening. My concern is that, once the pressure seemed to be off, as a nation we slid back to status quo. But then, I understand it's not easy to live faith in bold ways day to day. Believe me, I understand.

Now, Elijah was bold. As God's prophet he had to dispense hard truth, which didn't win him any votes with the folks of his day. Elijah didn't flinch even when he had to hide in the rocks to avoid certain death. Or when he came out of hiding to face ungodly priests, which he did with fervor and flames.

But a time did come when Elijah's faith waned, which just

between you and me made him someone I felt I could identify with in my own gyrating trust. Interestingly, the incident came after his victory against the priests. Instead of putting on a big victor's hoopla, we find Elijah hightailing it out of town, scared to death when Jezebel threatened his life.

Faith, like the face of a mountain, can be rocky, making the ascent tough. Any mountain climber will tell you that if you can't blindly trust the other climbers in the group to at times be your eyes and your strength, you'll never reach the summit. The same is true of faith. We must trust blindly what God is doing when we can't see beyond the overhang of our circumstances.

Sometimes I have more questions than answers, and maybe that's part of faith. I've noticed the more I know—or at least think I know—the more in control I feel. It becomes natural to rely on myself instead of on God. Conversely, the less I can depend on my intelligence and reasoning, the more I either have to live in fear because I don't know what's next or live in faith because I've relinquished my rights to have the script in my hands.

I've decided faith wasn't given to us to be logical but to be lived. While faith is grounded in truth, it is also swathed in mystery, and I'll never be able to figure it out in the same way I do my taxes or my checkbook. I have to trust the Lord's tally even when my faith seems no larger than a speck on the landscape of my life.

~ *Lord Jesus, I appreciate that I can bring all my ruminations, my questions, and even my doubts to you without fear of con-*

demnation. When my thoughts are askew, you use your Word to draw me back onto the right path. Grow in me a sturdy faith so that whether I am in the basins or on the mountaintops of life, I will stand strong for you. I am grateful, Lord, that you can take the tiniest seed of faith and cause it to burst forth in boldness. Amen.

# He Sings Over You

SHEILA WALSH

~

*The LORD your God is with you,*
*he is mighty to save.*
*He will take great delight in you,*
*he will quiet you with his love,*
*he will rejoice over you with singing. (Zephaniah 3:17)*

I LOVE TO SING TO MY SON, CHRISTIAN. I love to write little songs just for him. He usually appreciates it or puts up with it, although there was that one night last year that will forever live in my laugh lines. Christian was five and . . . let me give you a little background first.

We have a commitment to travel together as a family. We've done that since Christian was six weeks old. It hasn't always been easy, especially when he was very small and we seemed to cart the entire contents of his nursery. But my son and husband and I are a package deal and plan to stay that way. In the winter of 2002, however, we made an exception. I was asked to fly to the West Coast to speak at a conference for pastors. It was going to be a quick trip. I was to fly in Sunday night, speak at breakfast on Monday morning, and fly back at lunchtime that same day. It seemed crazy to make the whole family fly nearly four thousand miles round-trip for a thirty-minute talk, so

Barry and I decided that he and Christian would stay home. It felt strange to get ready to fly with no toys or crayons or books with a word count under 1,000. I felt a little lost.

"It'll be good for you," Barry reassured me. "You'll enjoy the break. You'll have the whole bed to yourself."

Well, I discovered that I didn't like it one little bit. I found myself in my hotel room that night talking to the television. In one horrified moment I realized that I am only one spouse and child away from being one of those strange people who mutters all the time, holding conversations with folks who have been gone for a long time.

Two long days later my plane touched down on Tennessee soil and I was home at last! When I walked in the back door, Christian threw himself into my arms. "I missed you so much, Mommy! Why didn't you take Daddy and me?"

"I thought it would be better for you to stay home, angel. It was a long trip." I hugged his neck, certain that he'd grown overnight.

"Well, you could have asked us!" he replied indignantly.

After his bath and prayers, I lay beside him telling him all about my trip. In a few minutes he closed his eyes and I began to sing to him softly. About two minutes into my sweet lullaby he patted my arm.

"I don't want to hurt your feelings, Mom, but I'm trying to sleep here!"

I laughed until my stomach ached. We both did. It took another thirty minutes to get him resettled. Absence might make the heart grow fonder, but the personality remains the same! Now that I was back where I belonged, my child just wanted to get on with the real stuff of life—like sleeping in peace without the diva of Nashville assaulting his ears!

Every time I think of that moment with Christian, I still laugh out loud. I think we are all like him at heart. We want our little world to be secure and predictable, but we don't want to miss anything either; we don't want to be left behind. We want to know that we are wanted and needed and loved and missed. We want to know that if we didn't show up, the party just wouldn't be the same. We want to be wrapped tenderly in love when we're lonely and left in peace when we've had enough. We want to go to sleep at night knowing all is well, that we can trust our heavenly parent to watch over us no matter what the next day may hold.

But real life isn't always so safe and tidy. My little boy knows it isn't. Before he turned five he'd already experienced the grief of losing two people he loved with all his heart: both his Nana and Papa died within two years of each other, leaving Christian with the questions every human being has to wrestle with time and again: Is the world a safe place for me to be? Can I trust the people I love not to leave me? Do I dare close my eyes, risk loving, embrace life as an adventure not to be missed, no matter what? Will God be there for me every moment of every day? *Is God good?*

Life is an open invitation to adventure for all. It's not only for the brave, but for the timid-hearted as well. It's a call to the Tomboy and the Tinkerbell. The great adventure of life in Christ is possible not because the world is "safe," but because our Father God is watching over us. We will never take a trip without him. We will never be left behind. We will never put our head down on a pillow at night and be alone. Our God is with us, where he belongs. He even sings over us—a love song so beautiful we will never want him to stop when we hear it with our hearts. Because of the security of his perfect love, we can be honest about where we are and dream of where we would like to go. Our fears and hopes are in our Father's safekeeping.

~ *Heavenly Father, sometimes the risks along the road to adventure seem too big for me . . . I'd rather play it safe. When I am afraid, remind me of the perfect security I have in you alone. Sing to me, Lord, until I can take the next step in front of me with trust in my heart. Amen.*

# Dreamin' of Heaven

BARBARA JOHNSON

~

*We know that if the earthly tent we live in is destroyed,*
*we have a building from God, an eternal house in heaven,*
*not built by human hands. Meanwhile we groan, longing to be*
*clothed with our heavenly dwelling. (2 Corinthians 5:1–2)*

DURING MY RECENT EXPERIENCE OF HAVING a cancerous brain tumor and central nervous system lymphoma, there were many days when I found that death was foremost in my mind. I sometimes felt that death was near, yet I never felt any fear or anxiety when those thoughts occurred. I only wished I had time to get some things in order (like cleaning out drawers and disposing of junk so my family wouldn't have a mess to sort through after my demise!).

Sometimes friends would get a little squeamish if I tried to talk about my feelings. "Oh, Barb, don't talk like that. You're not going to die anytime soon," they would say—then quickly change the subject.

It's almost as if we're embarrassed to talk about dying, but we shouldn't be. Instead, we should think of it as a grand adventure, an amazing change of address from pain to paradise. C. S. Lewis wrote in *Letters to an American Lady,* "There's nothing discreditable in dying. I've known the most respectable people to do it."

Let's face it: *Life* is a sexually transmitted, *terminal* condition. We're *all* going to die. And many of us will be observed during our deaths by family and friends who gather for our heavenly send-off. With that audience focused so intently on our every gesture and expression, we need to be aware, if possible, that the way we face death can show others the evidence of our faith. In fact, our greatest witness might come in our last moments on Earth.

I heard of a woman who suffered with a long, incapacitating illness. During the early stages of the disease, she was often grumpy and irritable toward those around her. But as her condition worsened and she became less communicative, an interesting thing happened. "She rarely spoke," her daughter said, "but she smiled a lot—more than she had ever smiled before."

Seeing their loved one smile on her deathbed made a strong impression on the woman's family members. "We believe she was at peace," her daughter said, "and that she was getting little glimpses of heaven. That was so reassuring to us and such a powerful witness."

Think of the two thieves who died on their crosses beside Jesus that terrible day on Golgotha. One of them hurled insults at the Lord. The other thief turned to Jesus in those last moments of his life. "Remember me when you come into your kingdom," he begged of the Lord (Luke 23:42).

I love Jesus' answer: *"Today* you will be with me in paradise" (v. 43, emphasis added).

Those are the same words he will whisper to us as we turn

to him in the last moments of our lives: "*Today* you will be with me . . . *Today!*"

After a lifetime of dreaming of my heavenly home, the promise that I'm about to meet Jesus in paradise will be the best news I've ever heard. Just thinking about getting to see Jesus face-to-face—and to see my two boys who have been there more than thirty years—fills me with joy. The seventeenth-century author John Milton wrote, "Death is the golden key that opens the palace of eternity."

I just hope, while I'm experiencing my final ecstatic moments of anticipation, my deathbed isn't surrounded by friends and family members who are mourning my condition! I've already put out the word: My death is to be a no-tears event. Instead, I've ordered my loved ones to serenade my departure with happy songs like "I'll Fly Away."

A friend of mine who has read my books and knows all about me recently admitted that she admired my faith but that she just couldn't quite bring herself to "believe in an after-life." She said she enjoyed reading my books, with all my joy-ful references to the life in heaven God has promised us, but she just couldn't accept the idea.

Then, a few days ago, she was diagnosed with breast cancer. Her first call after the diagnosis was to me. She said, "I really would like to know more about the possibility of life after death."

I was glad to share God's promises with her again, marveling at how quickly folks can change their theology when their personal mountains suddenly get steeper. The experience reminded me that we should all live our lives in ways that can influence others whenever we have the opportunity. You never know when the phone might ring and a friend might say, "Okay, I'm ready. Tell me about your friend Jesus."

To know we have the promise of eternal life with Jesus is worth all the pain in this world. As someone said, "Earth has no sorrow that heaven cannot heal." What a privilege we have to share that truth in the way we live—or in the way we die.

~ *Dear God, thank you for the faith I have and the assurance your Word gives me that I have eternal life, that my future is positive and forever secure in you. Amen.*

# CONCLUSION

## *The Train Conductor*

### THELMA WELLS

~

THE PASSENGER TRAIN RAN FROM OUR neighborhood to downtown Dallas in the l940s and 1950s. As a little girl I would board the train near my home at Knox Street and enjoy the ride downtown because I completely trusted my grandfather, who was the conductor. "Daddy Lawrence" would even take me to work with him on Saturdays when I'd spend the weekends with him and my grandmother.

I had learned to love and trust my maternal grandfather because we enjoyed many adventures together. On some weekends we would go to the Majestic Theater and sit in the balcony called the "buzzard roost," the only place black people were allowed to sit in the movie house during the Jim Crow years. That was an adventure. On other days together, Daddy Lawrence would send me off on a local train ride. I loved to ride the train and listen to the bell ring and feel the clatter of the steel wheels on the thick old rails.

The scenery was always fascinating because I got to see the massive, beautifully landscaped mansions on the edge of Highland Park and University Park. I daydreamed about living and shopping in this fancy community that surely had to be inhabited by rich people.

When I would get to the end of the ride, everything I thought I understood became murky, however, because my grandfather, whom I thought I'd left on Knox Street, was always standing at the train station with his blue-and-white-striped cap on his head and the red, Texas-style bandanna tied around his neck, waiting for me. How in the world did he get there, watching me get off the train when I had left him miles behind?

I experienced this great mystery for several years, and I never figured out until I was grown with children of my own that Daddy Lawrence was in the front car of the train when we left Knox Street, and I was in the end car. He would leap off the train when it pulled into the downtown depot and stand at attention, beaming at me when I arrived. I always looked forward to seeing him standing there, smiling at me and saying, "Hi, Pooch. Did you enjoy the ride?" It didn't matter that I could never figure out this geographical puzzle. All I knew was that my grandfather cared for me and would never let anything bad happen to me. He had already proved that by protecting me in so many ways—including no longer allowing me to spend time alone with my grandmother, who put me in a closet when he wasn't at home. I trusted Daddy Lawrence in spite of the fact that I didn't understand how he got to the depot before I did. I just knew he would be waiting for me—wherever the ride took me.

That's the way it is with me and God. He's the Conductor on my train of life. I don't understand how he's always in my mind, keeping my dreams alive about what could be, may be, shall be. I don't understand how he can be everywhere at once, always smiling at me and seeing after me. I do know that I have learned to trust God in every arena of my life, even more than I ever trusted Daddy Lawrence . . . and that's saying a lot! As great as my grandfather's ability was to conduct my childhood affairs, my heavenly Father's capacity and care are infinitely greater. God is my Conductor for life, keeping me protected and showing me how to enjoy the ride. Sometimes, when I feel like the brakes on the train are failing, I close my eyes . . . and next thing I know, I see him standing at the depot, beaming at me and welcoming me to safety.

"In hard traveling year in and year out," wrote the apostle Paul, "I've had to ford rivers, fend off robbers, struggle with friends, struggle with foes. I've been at risk in the city, at risk in the country, endangered by desert sun and sea storm, and betrayed by those I thought were my brothers" (2 Corinthians 11:26 MSG). As we go down life's tracks from point B (birth) to point D (death), many scenes beckon us. Many struggles cause us to feel at risk. Many mysteries occur and many precious encounters await. All are adventures on the route of life. At the beginning, in the middle, and at the end of the journey, there is the Conductor, Jesus, assuring us that he is participating in every mile of the ride. Because of his sovereignty and unfathomable love, we can relax, sit back, and enjoy the excursion. We are divinely led.

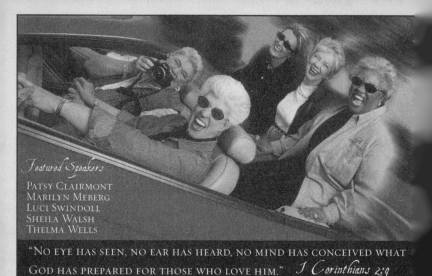

*Featured Speakers*

PATSY CLAIRMONT
MARILYN MEBERG
LUCI SWINDOLL
SHEILA WALSH
THELMA WELLS

"NO EYE HAS SEEN, NO EAR HAS HEARD, NO MIND HAS CONCEIVED WHAT GOD HAS PREPARED FOR THOSE WHO LOVE HIM." *I Corinthians 2:9*

# THOUSANDS OF WOMEN ARE GATHERING FOR A LIFE-CHANGING EXPERIENCE.

*The* GREAT *Adventure* *June 2003*

## The Great Adventure 2003 Dates*

February 21–22
Sacramento, CA
ARCO Arena

March 14–15
Memphis, TN
Pyramid Arena

March 28–29
Columbus, OH
Nationwide Arena

April 4–5
Kansas City, MO
Kemper Arena

April 25–26
Vancouver, BC
General Motors Place

May 2–3
Shreveport, LA
CenturyTel Center

May 16–17
Louisville, KY
Kentucky Fair & Expo Ctr

May 30–31
Billings, MT
MetraPark

June 6-7
Anaheim, CA
Arrowhead Pond

June 13–14
Charleston, SC
N. Charleston Coliseum

June 20–21
Ft. Lauderdale, FL
Office Depot Center

June 27–28
Washington, DC
MCI Center

July 11–12
Dallas, TX
America Airlines Ctr

July 18–19
Toronto/Hamilton, ON
Copps Coliseum

July 25–26
Denver, CO
Pepsi Center

August 1–2
Atlanta, GA
Philips Arena

August 8–9
Oklahoma City, OK
Ford Center

August 15–16
Ames, IA
Hilton Coliseum

August 22–23
Chicago, IL
United Center

September 5–6
Anaheim, CA
Arrowhead Pond

September 12–13
St. Paul, MN
Xcel Energy Center

September 19–20
Albany, NY
Pepsi Arena

September 26–27
Detroit, MI
Palace of Auburn Hills

October 3-4
Hartford, CT
Hartford Civic Center

October 10–11
Portland, OR
Rose Garden Arena

October 24–25
Charlotte, NC
Charlotte Coliseum

October 31–November
Omaha, NE
Omaha Conv Ctr & Ar

November 7–8
Philadelphia, PA
First Union Center

November 14–15
Orlando, FL
TD Waterhouse Centre

* Dates and locatio
subject to change.

WOMEN OF FAITH®
A Division of Thomas Nelson, Inc.

For more information call **1-888-49-FAITH**
or visit us on the web at **womenoffaith.com**